L I F E L O N G
CAREER PLANNING

LIFELONG CAREER PLANNING

John Milton Dillard
Texas A&M University

CHARLES E. MERRILL PUBLISHING COMPANY
A BELL & HOWELL COMPANY
COLUMBUS   TORONTO   LONDON   SYDNEY

Published by Charles E. Merrill Publishing Co.
A Bell & Howell Company
Columbus, Ohio 43216

This book was set in Serifa
Cover Design Coordination: Cathy Watterson
Cover Art: Steve Botts
Text Design: Ben Shriver
Production Coordination: Ben Shriver

Library of Congress Catalog Card Number: 84-43020
International Standard Book Number: 0-675-20348-1
Printed in the United States of America
  2 3 4 5 6 7 8 9 10—89 88 87 86

To my mother
Mrs. Lucy Scott
and in memory of my stepfather
Mr. Alonzo Scott

PREFACE

Lifelong Career Planning is designed for students to use in career planning courses, vocational and career information courses, and career development theory courses. This text introduces skills which students can use throughout their careers. Career planning and decision making, both ongoing processes, are integral parts of the text. Persons who are developing or reassessing their career goals will find this book invaluable. Therefore, it can be used by various college students—those entering college immediately after high school as well as those entering at later periods; those attending community/junior colleges, four-year colleges, and universities, as well as those who are shifting gears at midlife.

Each chapter of the nine chapters contains several special appropriately placed features called "Tips for Self-Assessment," which ask you to apply the concepts discussed in that section of the text. These features engage the reader in thoughtful consideration of the main ideas in every chapter. Also in every chapter many examples illustrate each key topic, to help the reader easily grasp the material. The text of each chapter ends with a summary of main points. Experiential exercises at the very end of each chapter allow the reader to further master career-planning skills.

This text is unique in that it is concerned with ongoing life planning and decision making. Practical career planning and decision-making skills are useful not only for obtaining a career, but for getting off to a good start in a new career, for maintaining a career and for switching to another career. Needless to say, the material presented in this text is of equal relevance to the career development of women and men.

Finally, this book was written for the Eighties—with a realization that adapting satisfactorily to the career market in these times of expanding options and never-ending changes is not always an easy task. This text was written for a variety of reasons, but a special reason was to provide adults of all ages with suggestions to make their work lives and their personal lives happier and more meaningful through effective career planning and decision making.

Many people assisted with the development of this book and offered suggestions for various chapters. I would especially like to thank two editors at Charles E. Merrill, Marianne Taflinger, who initially suggested my developing this book, and Vicki Knight, for her exceptional patience, continuous support, and encouragement.

Bonnie Salim, who read the complete first draft, made valued editorial suggestions.

Thanks also to Marti Rice and Evelyn Ferchau, who labored unstintingly in typing the manuscript through its various phases.

I am grateful to the reviewers for their constructive and helpful suggestions throughout the development of the manuscript: Jennifer White, Lansing Community College; Velma Walker, Tarrant County Junior College; Ned A. Katterheinrich, Columbus Technical Institute; Marsha Julian, Cuyahoga Community College; Patricia D. Cavico, Broward Community College; Mary Laing, Lansing Community College; Gerald Floyd, Santa Barbara Community College; John Schick, Lakeland Community College; James C. Jokerst, Aims Community College; Steve Bundy, Chabot College; and Karen Casanares, Skyline College.

Finally, thanks to Dr. Victor R. Lindquist, who gave permission to reprint a portion of the *Northwestern Endicott Report.*

My most sincere appreciation to all of you!

CONTENTS

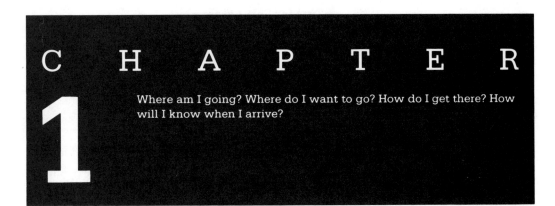

C H A P T E R

1

Where am I going? Where do I want to go? How do I get there? How will I know when I arrive?

Career Planning

Some people have jobs, others have careers. What is the difference? A fine line divides the two, but generally, the word *job* refers to work which lacks continuity and may be temporary.

The classic example of an individual who has a job is Ned who mixes and carries mortar to bricklayers two days a week, mows lawns on weekends, bags and carries groceries at the local supermarket evenings, and paints houses during the spring and summer. Although Ned works, he clearly does not have a career, only a job that demands little skill, education, or dedication.

The word *career*, on the other hand, implies training and commitment, such as in the fields of engineering, medicine, or education. You would be mistaken to think a bachelor's degree or higher is necessary to have a career. A career is what you choose to do as your life's work. It is also a path which you purposely choose to take you closer to your ideal form of work. A career implies success in what you have chosen to do and an accompanying sense of personal and financial well-being.

Tips for Self-Assessment

- Now that I understand the difference between a *job* and a *career*, should I establish a goal of planning a career or finding a job?
- Since many jobs existing today will be nonexistent by the 1990s, how will I tailor my career plans for the future?
- How important is having a career to me?

Although well-paid in her position as a typing teacher, Jennie wanted a greater challenge. Because she was good at supervising others, she began working in business management at a telephone company and felt satisfied directing other employees. Jennie then had a career.

While in high school, Tom started working summers with a construction company. He soon recognized that he would not use his skills in drafting unless he enrolled in drafting courses and undertook only those jobs involving drafting while he was a student. His experiences could then bring him closer to his goal of working in the construction company's drafting department.

Before launching a career, you need to assess your needs and interests, make plans for attaining your career goals, and then work to achieve those goals. You might begin by asking yourself the following questions.

What kind of work do I want to perform for the rest of my life? Where are my current work experiences taking me? Are there any paths to the ideal career? If I did attain my ideal position, would I recognize it? Unfortunately, many adults do not have firm answers to these questions. Many began careers with only vague ideas about their goals and how they could achieve them. Year after year too many adults either unhappily stay in the same job or move from one job to the next experiencing little, if any, personal or financial satisfaction. This sad situation occurs because many people do not focus on their goals and, even more importantly, do not plan how they can achieve them.

GOALS IN CAREER PLANNING

Tips for Self-Assessment

- In order to achieve a successful career, which of my needs and desires do I need to meet?
- Why should I consider career planning a lifelong process?

Your major rationale for working is to earn a living. In addition, you may strive to attain a personal goal or work for a specific purpose. Perhaps the personal, social, and/or economic aspects of your life are changing. You may in turn need to change your career goals. Along with many others in a similar position, you may decide to seek career assistance.

Through this assistance you frequently attain self-awareness and self-understanding, personal satisfaction, adequate placement, and efficient use of time and effort.

ACQUIRING SELF-AWARENESS AND UNDERSTANDING

Appraisal of your strengths and weaknesses is an important step in career planning. Such an assessment enables you to better understand yourself in relation to your career goals and plans. The results of this assessment will allow you to realistically evaluate yourself and help you appropriately apply your knowledge to career planning.

You may avoid dissatisfaction, disappointment, and unhappiness through accurate self-awareness. By understanding yourself, you may achieve intelligent, efficient direction in your life and can begin to manage difficulties which may occur within your lifetime. Finally, as you better understand and accept yourself, you establish a foundation for understanding and accepting other people.

ATTAINING PERSONAL SATISFACTION

Achieving personal satisfaction from your career is one goal in career planning. Since you spend much of your life working, you should select a career which will yield the highest return in personal satisfaction. You are likely to prefer career activities that are similar to your interests or that give you emotional and/or physical pleasure. To derive satisfaction from your life's work, you must understand the requirements of your career and recognize your interests and desires.

If you generally enjoy life, you probably will be satisfied with your career. Or, more specifically, if you are happy with everyday occurrences, you deal with work positively. When you feel satisfied with work, you are likely to express a positive attitude toward other aspects of your life. Probably, to attain personal satisfaction, you seek more than just adequate pay and other tangible rewards. Factors which contribute to your satisfaction may be working conditions, challenges, and interpersonal relationships.

Some studies suggest that less educated, unskilled, and younger workers experience less job satisfaction than do many professional–technical workers, officials, and independent business owners. However, more than three-quarters of Americans surveyed have responded that they are satisfied with their career.[1]

---

[1]Robert P. Quinn, Graham L. Staines, and Margaret R. McCullough, "Job Satisfaction: Is There a Trend?" *Manpower Research*, U.S. Department of Labor, no. 30. (Washington, D.C., 1974).

PREPARING FOR ADEQUATE PLACEMENT

Part of your goal in career planning will be attaining work for which you feel adequately prepared. Hopefully you will seek work that appears almost custom-designed. How can you achieve suitable career placement? During career planning, you may want to avoid areas which provide limited opportunities or are not suited to your interests. It is equally important to invest less time and energy with those careers you identify as beyond the limits of your abilities.

Throughout career planning, focus your attention on those careers that best suit you. Appraise your assets and liabilities and compare them with the requirements for various careers. Such an approach will help you find a career for which you will be adequately prepared.

EFFICIENTLY USING TIME AND EFFORT

Another goal of career planning is to enable you to systematically select a career. Systematic planning will help you avoid trial-and-error methods and help you spend more time working toward your stated goals.

You can efficiently use your time by studying yourself in relation to various careers. Generally, persons who have participated in career planning are more satisfied with their careers and remain employed longer than those who have not.

STEPS IN CAREER PLANNING

Tips for Self-Assessment

- If I am a college student, am I adequately planning for my career after graduation?
- If I have already searched for a job and am working, why do I need to study career planning?
- How will systematic career planning help me enter (reenter) the marketplace or switch careers?
- How can a career specialist help me?

Attaining success through career planning is not simple; many steps are necessary. If you engage in a step-by-step procedure, you can better focus your efforts on each stage of the process. Admittedly, you might be successful without having followed a gradual planning procedure. Generally, your planning will furnish you with valuable personal information. Achieving success in career planning begins with examining your aptitudes, interests, personality, values, career opportunities, performance, and lifestyle.

tomorrow's career success

| HEALTH |
| WEALTH |
| HAPPINESS |
| FRIENDS |
| GROWTH |
| PEACE |
| SECURITY |
| LEISURE |
| FREEDOM |
| OPPORTUNITY |

today's career success

TEMPORARILY OUT OF SERVICE
Please use the stairs

YOUR LIFESTYLE

YOUR CAREER PERFORMANCE

YOUR CAREER OPPORTUNITIES

YOUR PERSONALITY

YOUR VALUES

YOUR INTERESTS

YOUR APTITUDES

Will you wait for
restored elevator service?
or
will you take the stairs?

FIGURE 1-1   **Steps in career planning**

YOUR APTITUDES

You begin career planning by analyzing your aptitudes or studying your undeveloped skills and natural talents. Through analysis you become aware of your mental and physical strengths and weaknesses. Such information helps you focus your attention on those careers requiring similar aptitudes; however, your possessing aptitudes in a particular career may not ensure your personal satisfaction. Aptitude provides only a basis for predicting the likelihood of your success in a specific career or training program.

Several measures determine aptitudes. A career counselor may suggest the *Army Services Vocational Aptitude Battery*, the *General Aptitude Test Battery*, the *Differential Aptitude Tests*, and the *Flanagan Aptitude Classification Tests*. The results of these and other measures may help you plan your career.

Consider Sue Ellen, a twenty year old college student who contacted the Career Information Center regarding her interest in medical laboratory technology. Although her mother, father, and sister were medical laboratory technologists, she was unsure of her aptitude for this career. A career specialist told Sue Ellen there were various skills used in medical laboratory technology and encouraged her to read about the field in the career center study area. After Sue Ellen reviewed the literature, the career counselor assessed her scholastic file and previous work experience. The counselor determined Sue Ellen had previously used three of the needed skills—numerical, spatial, and perceptual aptitudes.

Thirty-six year old Sam, a construction manager, considered becoming a high school mathematics teacher. Sam took aptitude test inventories to learn whether he had the abilities of a math teacher. The results of the aptitude test suggested that he lacked sufficient numerical and spatial reasoning and form perception. Sam found he needed to explore other positions as part of his career plan.

Patricia, a forty-two year old displaced homemaker, planned to attend a community college but was unsure of which field to enter. She had worked for only one and a half years in an office shortly after finishing high school. Although she had some clerical experience, she did not want to work in clerical or secretarial areas. Patricia took three measurement inventories, including a battery of aptitude tests. Using the results, a counselor helped Patricia determine her assets and liabilities and later helped her explore various career areas.

YOUR INTERESTS

Not only must you have aptitude for a given field but also interests in that area. Conflicting interests may make it difficult for a person to identify her interest pattern. She may desire a particular kind of work, be well acquainted with it, and yet, still have some misgivings about whether she is truly interested; however, the higher the relationship between career interests and aptitudes, the greater the probability a person will be successful in a career.

Career specialists and counselors use several measures to identify career interests and to assist career planning, such as the *Strong-Campbell Interest Inventory, Kuder Occupational Interest Survey, Self-Directed Search, Sex Bias and Sex Fairness in Interest Assessment, Harrington/O'Shea Systems for Career Decision-Making, Minnesota Vocational Interest Inventory,* and *Non-Sexist Vocational Card Sort.* These inventories can provide a systematic method for considering interest patterns.

Ratings on an interest inventory might vary from one career field to another. For instance, you might have high scores on mechanical, computational, and scientific areas, but low scores on other career areas that require different combinations of interests. Although an interest inventory cannot tell you exactly what career you should follow, it can, together with other information, assist you in narrowing down your range of career choices.

YOUR VALUES

For work to be satisfying it must generally agree with a person's value system. Individuals tend to seek careers that allow them to be who they want to be. You reveal your values when you say something you feel is worthwhile or when you act on a firm belief. Your words and actions reflect your aspirations and may direct your decisions. When your actions are consistent with your values, you usually feel happy for being honest to yourself. On the other hand, you may feel anxious when your behavior is not consistent with your values. Assessing whether certain kinds of work are meaningful, challenging, or honest depends on your values.

A person derives his values from his internal needs, which he feels he must satisfy. To plan successfully, he should identify and clarify his values in relation to specific careers, home environment, significant others, and leisure time. Career specialists and counselors use several measures to identify career values. Some examples are *Survey of Interpersonal Values, Bowling Green University Survey of Work Values, Rokeach Values Survey, Study of Values,* and *Work Environment Preference Schedules.* Consider how the following individuals used these values inventories.

Robert, middle-aged and single, sought help at the career counseling center regarding his need for a satisfying career environment. To determine some of his likes and dislikes about work, Robert took the *Bowling Green University Survey of Work Values.* The results indicated that Robert valued a strong personal attitude toward high earnings, pride in work, and responsibility to work. His career specialist shared this information with him to initiate his exploration of various careers. Robert studied many career options to find out which were consistent with his values.

Grace, a twenty year old, first-year student, was majoring in medical technology at El Centro Community College. Although she first felt medical laboratory technology would allow her to develop her full potential, she decided to change her major area of study. The career counselor selected the *Survey of Interpersonal Values* and administered it to her. The results suggested that Grace valued independence, recognition, and leadership. Her ratings of these values provided Grace with more information about herself, encouraging her to explore a wider range of other career fields as part of her career planning.

YOUR PERSONALITY

While planning a career, you should consider your personality; that is, what motivates you and how you relate to other people. Having the necessary aptitudes, values, and interests may help you in your career, but just as important, you must have personality traits which the career requires. Consider Scott, who had the aptitudes, values, and interests of an insurance agent but failed in the field because he was unable to maintain a schedule and effectively persuade his clients to buy policies. Personality may make the difference between success or failure in a specific position or career.

Strix Pix

A job.

Self-awareness can help you to make appropriate adjustments in career planning. Personality inventories such as the *Edwards Personal Preference Schedule, Sixteen Personality Factor Questionnaire, California Test of Personality, Omnibus Personality Inventory*, and *Guilford-Zimmermans Temperament Survey* help you achieve this knowledge. The following examples show how individuals used these and other inventories to become better acquainted with themselves.

Maria, thirty-four years old and single, told the career counselor she was having difficulties at work. These difficulties affected her relationships with her fiancé, close relatives, and friends. Although during her first year, Maria performed well as a consular officer in the foreign services, she had been working less enthusiastically during the past eight months. Maria completed a personality schedule, and the results suggested that she had a high desire to achieve. Various tasks which had initially interested her had become boring. Having expressed her concerns, Maria decided to change to either the political or administrative affairs areas of the foreign services.

Strix Pix

A career.

Upon entering community college, nineteen year old Alberto wanted to become a police officer. After talking with the career specialist, Alberto completed a personality inventory. The results suggested he was restrained, prefered to make his own decisions, followed impulses, and was change-able. Alberto felt the results accurately described his behavior. He realized these qualities would not make him an effective police officer. Alberto either had to change his personality to fit his desired career or explore other careers more consistent with his personality.

YOUR CAREER OPPORTUNITIES

Just having the necessary personality, values, interests, and skills and aptitudes will not ensure you an opportunity to perform in your preferred career. You may only get the chance to work in an area where you are neither qualified nor skilled. Or, you may not identify the right opportunities when they arise. Some career opportunities do happen by chance, but you need to learn about potential jobs which may use your talents and how to present yourself to employers. You must be able to communicate your potential skills, abilities, and talents to those who are hiring. Systematic planning *can* enhance your career opportunities.

YOUR CAREER PERFORMANCE

Your career performance should be consistent with the rules or behaviors employers or professionals expect. Knowing their standards will help you establish yourself on the job. Standards differ from one career or business to the next; therefore, you must learn how your employer evaluates performance. Of equal importance is acquiring the "know-how" to improve your performance.

YOUR LIFESTYLE

What is your lifestyle? Your lifestyle might be described by one or more of the following phrases: (a) acquires (or lacks) money and high status, (b) provides for leisure time and pleasure, (c) plans for future financial security, (d) moves to different geographical locations and travels frequently, (e) spends time on community and civic projects, (f) commands or makes all-important decisions, and (g) values accomplishments through education.

Successful career planning hinges on how well you integrate your way of life with the options which are open to you. Ignoring your lifestyle may limit your achievement. You may start a career for which you have been well-trained, but your lifestyle may not fit the career's requirements. For instance, you might have to work during hot summer months; work overtime, evenings, or weekends; work in a location away from your family; or work in groups where others make most of the decisions.

You should also consider how your lifestyle might change in the future. You may now be single, independent, achieving high goals, and frequently traveling, but five to ten years later you may be married and have children. To accommodate such changes, you may have to alter your lifestyle.

In summary, you may benefit the most from career planning if you assess each rung on the ladder of success and apply each to yourself. Whether you are just starting a new job or considering a career change, systematic planning will help ensure the outcome you seek.

Having just studied the steps in career planning, you are ready to begin writing your own plan. Start by getting a pencil and paper. Then take a moment to review Figure 1–2.

Read the following questions and write your answers on your planning sheet.

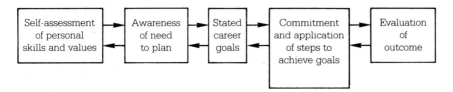

FIGURE 1–2   **Systematic process model to career planning**

1. List and evaluate your skills and values.
2. Write several reasons why you personally need to plan a career path.
3. Clearly state your lifetime goals. Then describe those specific goals you wish to accomplish in the near future.
4. Identify the steps you must take to attain your goals.

Save this initial planning sheet. Later, after starting a career, return to the sheet. Consider the final step of Figure 1–2, *Evaluation of outcome*. If at that time you haven't achieved your stated aims, consider readjusting your goals.

Usually, people who accomplish great things do not blunder into achievement. They have planned. Planning requires thinking, and, as a rule, the more logical the thinking, the sounder the plan. While it is essential to know where you are going, knowing what to do once you get there is equally important.

BENEFITS FROM CAREER PLANNING

Tips for Self-Assessment

- **How successful can I be without a career plan?**
- **How will I benefit from planning my career?**

Anyone who wants a successful career at some point needs to have a career plan. Some individuals succeed without one because of special circumstances in their lives (such as knowing the right people and getting special breaks); others are not so fortunate and must make their own opportunities. They do this by taking control of their lives and determining whether they will be happy in a chosen job.

Career planning can benefit individuals entering a career after graduation or those returning to work after a prolonged absence. It can also benefit individuals who are changing careers either by their own choice (job dissatisfaction) or by circumstances beyond their control (layoffs or retirement).

Not only do you plan when you are beginning a career, you do so periodically through your lifetime in response to change. Such planning is referred to in this text as *lifelong career planning.* Lifelong career planning takes into account how you and society will change in the coming years. Now you may be planning a career for the near future, but you are likely to have future social and economic needs based on change.

Scott had planned to become an independent insurance agent. Following his training, he went into the insurance business for himself. Business was great at the outset, but the number of clients began to decrease after the first three years. Scott decided to switch to a new career with hopes of earning more money. What career should he have switched to? Sue, a homemaker with four children, wanted to work outside her home as a business manager. Could she succeed in the business world? Jack was sixty-four and would soon retire. He would have leisure time on his hands. What should he do with it? How prepared were Scott, Sue, and Jack to adjust to the changes in their lives? What skills could they have identified, developed, or learned to have dealt with such changes?

Through career planning, you can improve your self-awareness and self-understanding (Chapters 1 and 2), acquire effective decision-making skills (Chapter 3), explore the marketplace and career fields (Chapters 4 and 5), learn how to locate a job and develop skills for success (Chapters 6 and 7), and improve your knowledge of lifelong career planning (Chapters 8 and 9).

Using lifelong career planning, you can identify your skills and continue to assess your needs. Planning must be considered continuous. You should design your present plan so that it will be adaptable to change and will provide sound alternatives for the future.

POINTS TO REVIEW

1. Generally people with *careers* have decided upon their life goals. Many people with *jobs* have not defined their goals as clearly. Everyone who participates in career planning must evaluate the advantages and disadvantages of having a career or job.

2. Deciding your own goals allows you to take control of your future. (Letting others make your decisions will not help you.)

3. Most young and mid-life adults benefit from systematic career planning. Benefits especially accrue for young adults and college students with career goals, mid-life adults re-entering the job market, or adults in the process of a planned or an unplanned career change.

4. Major benefits of career planning are (a) improved self-awareness and self-understanding, (b) knowledge of various career fields, (c) effective decision-making skills, (d) information pointing towards the location of available careers, and (e) skills for marketing yourself.

5. Effective career planning involves assessing personal skills and values, planning, stating career goal(s), and committing yourself to the goal(s), applying steps to achieve the goal(s), and evaluating the results.

6. Career planning is lifelong. As your lifestyle changes, so will your career plans.

7. Major goals of career planning include self-understanding, personal satisfaction, preparing for adequate placement and financial rewards, effectively using time, and attaining personal and career success.

8. In order to plan productively you must examine your aptitudes, interests, values, personality, career opportunities, career performance, and life-style.

Experiential Exercises

Read situations *1.* and *2.* and respond to the questions that follow.

1. Nineteen year old Sam completed high school a year ago and still does not know what he would like to do with his life. Currently he works at a local retail food market as a carry-out clerk. Sam lives with his parents but really wants to be on his own.

    a. How would you describe Sam's situation?

    b. What would you do differently if you were Sam?

    c. How might career planning help Sam?

2. Donna, middle-aged and also married, has a twenty-three year old daughter who lives with her. Donna has been working for a local IBM branch as an administrative assistant for the past fifteen years. Recently she has felt frustrated at work and angry at the company. She does not like her position at work or some of the things she is required to do there. Donna feels she can no longer accept the company's practices, although she once accepted or at least tolerated them.

    a. What do you perceive is Donna's major problem?

    b. What would you do if you were Donna?

    c. Can career planning help Donna? Explain.

3. Assume that the timeline below is a framework of your life.

    a. Fantasize and describe how your career or life may change as you move from the teenage years to retirement.

    b. How might career planning help you through the different stages on the timeline to face career or life changes?

4. List advantages of developing a systematic career plan.

    a.

    b.

    c.

    d.

    e.

    f.

5. Describe how you would use the seven steps (aptitudes, interests, values, personality, lifestyle, career opportunities, and career performance) in career planning.

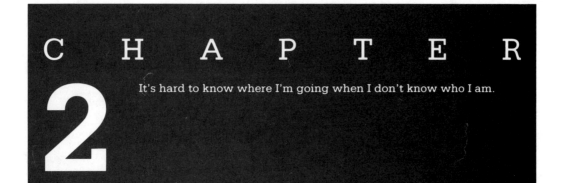

C H A P T E R

2

It's hard to know where I'm going when I don't know who I am.

Increasing Self-Knowledge

Change best describes the world of work today. Adults of all ages must prepare themselves to deal with change. Throughout your lifetime you may make a number of career choices. One expert has reported that a high percentage of workers who were heads of households worked in five different positions during their lifetime.[1]

Increased work status, higher earning power, improved working conditions, or increased work security may lead to these changes. Yet, the major reason individuals shift to other types of work is the rapidly changing nature of the labor market. Thousands of jobs have been eliminated; others now require new skills. At the same time new career fields are starting. Scientists have created robots, computers, computer operated lathes and drill presses, and numerically controlled machines which are increasingly replacing human workers. Look forward to a lifetime of career choices. The position you choose or are hired to fill today may become obsolete within a few years.

Consider your present career choice the beginning of a series of closely-related choices. When you are relatively young, you will make initial

[1]H. W. Bernard and D. W. Fullmer, *Principles of Guidance,* 2nd ed. (New York: Thomas Y. Crowell, 1977).

decisions and will continue choosing alternatives throughout most of your life. You need to know the factors which will influence your career choices as they occur.

Tips for Self-Assessment

- How did I decide to enter my current career field?
- What factors influenced my career development?
- How conscious am I of the factors influencing my career?
- Which of these factors were under my control and which were not?
- Will I be able to control any of these factors in the future?

Why have you decided on a particular field as you begin your life's work? Perhaps you have not made up your mind about a specific career. Have you considered the reasons why you are undecided? Your response might be that since you were a child, you have wanted to be an elementary school teacher, an accountant, or an engineer. You might answer that choosing a career in the insurance field would be following a family career tradition. Perhaps you may say you are not sure how you got where you are—it just happened! However, being aware of those persons or things that help to shape your career choice can assist you in making a realistic selection.

PERSONALITY AND YOUR CAREER CHOICE

To choose your career without having considered your personality may be unwise. Eventually, knowing why you chose your career, knowing what factors determined your choice, may be more beneficial than your actual choices. Throughout your life your work may change due to shifting personal needs, desires, and motives. Moreover, your curiosity, desire to perform, need to control your surroundings, or wish to improve your working conditions may spur you into making another career choice.

Making a realistic career choice, or in some situations re-selecting a career, is one of the most important tasks an adult faces. In the sections that follow, we'll look at what authorities say about factors that shape your career choice.

CAREER SELF-CONCEPT

Your career decisions and how you go about making them serve as at least a partial basis for how you see yourself, according to Donald E. Super.[2]

---

[2]Donald E. Super, "Vocational Development Theory: Persons, Positions, and Processes," in *Perspectives on Vocational Development*, ed. J. M. Whiteley and A. Rasniknoff (Washington, DC: American Personnel and Guidance Association, 1972), 13–33.

Tips for Self-Assessment

- What is my perception of myself in a career?
- How consistent is this career self-concept with my mental and physical abilities?
- How has my career self-concept influenced what I want as my life's work?

Whether accurate or inaccurate, self-statements are important because they prompt you to prescribe your vocational limits. While initially focusing on a career or career change, a person may state, "I am not smart enough to study electronics," or "I believe that I am good at political science. I'm sure to become a corporate attorney." A person may think, "I have a firm position with IBM as senior computer engineer, but after twenty years of service I'm not sure I can compete much longer with my young assistants who seem eager to replace me." Perhaps a man might say, "I have always wanted to be a realtor, particularly now that my two daughters have gone to college."

Frequently you act upon your feelings concerning who you are, what you desire to become, what you can become, how your situation may change, and how you perceive the relationship between yourself and your situation. In point of fact, how you arrive at a self-statement, as well as the statement itself, influences your career choice.

Tips for Self-Assessment

- How consistent is Super's self-concept theory with my own career development?
- How different was my career self-concept at nineteen from what is is now?

Super theorizes that you select a career which enables you to have a role consistent with your career self-concept. He believes your career self-concept forms as you pass through a series of life stages. Super and Jordaan[3] summarize the career stages and the tasks of each stage as follows:

1. *Growth stage* (birth–14). Self-concept develops through identification with key figures in family and in school. Needs and fantasy are dominant early in this stage, and interest and capacity become more important with increasing social participation and reality testing. Substages of the growth stage are:

   Fantasy (4–10). Needs are dominant; role-playing in fantasy is important.

   Interest (11–12). Likes are the major determinant of aspirations and activities.

---

[3]Donald E. Super, and Jean Pierre Jordaan, "Career Development Theory," *British Journal of Guidance and Counseling*, 1 (October, 1973): 3–16.

Capacity (13–14). Abilities are given more weight, and career requirements, including training, are considered.

2. *Exploration stage* (age 15–24). Self-examination, role try-outs, and occupational exploration take place in school, leisure activities, and part-time work. Sub-stages of the exploration stage are:

Tentative (15–17). Needs, interests, capacities, values, and opportunities are all considered. Tentative choices are made and tried out in fantasy, discussion, courses, work, etc.

Transition (18–21). Reality considerations are given more weight as the youth enters the labor market or professional training and attempts to implement a self-concept.

Trial—little commitment (22–24). A seemingly appropriate field having been located, a first work role in it is found and is tried out as a potential life work.

3. *Establishment stage* (age 25–44). Having found an appropriate field, the person makes an effort to establish a permanent place in it. There may be some trial early in this stage, with consequent shifting, but establishment may begin without trial, especially in the professions. Substages of the establishment stage are:

Trial—*commitment and stabilization* (25–30). The field of work presumed to be suitable may prove unsatisfactory, resulting in one or two changes before the life work is found or before it becomes clear that the life work will be a succession of unrelated career activities.

Advancement (31–44). As the career pattern becomes clear, effort is put forth to stabilize and to make a secure place in the world of work. For most persons, these are the creative years.

4. *Maintenance stage* (age 45–64). Having made a place in the world of work, the concern is now to hold it. Little ground is broken, but there is continuation along established lines.

5. *Decline stage* (age 65 on). As physical and mental powers decline, work activity changes and in due course ceases. New roles must be developed—first that of selective participant and then that of observer. Substages of this stage are:

Deceleration (65–70). Sometimes at the time of official retirement, sometimes late in the maintenance stage, the pace of work slackens, duties are shifted, or the nature of the work is changed to suit declining capacities. Many persons find part-time work to replace their full-time career.

Retirement (71 on). As with all the specified age limits, there are great variations from person to person. But complete cessation of a career comes for all in due course—to some easily and pleasantly, to others with difficulty and disappointment, and to some only with death.

Super and Jordaans' sequence of career developmental tasks (from the exploration through the decline stages of development) appears in Table 2–1. Notice that tasks can occur at age levels other than those listed.

These developmental tasks encompass a broad perspective of attitudes and behaviors within each stage of development. The *crystallization* task requires that you establish a preferred plan and consider how you can put it into action. This task also includes developing career self-concepts. The concepts will enable you to make a tentative career choice after reflecting upon your feelings and other information concerning who you are. The task of *specification* requires that you make a specific career choice by narrowing a broad career interest into a single one. *Implementation* calls for attaining necessary training and entering your chosen career field. The task of *stabilization* involves settling down in your career field and applying your talents and skills. As part of this task a person may shift to other positions within the field but seldom to another career field. During *advancement* you obtain seniority, demonstrate superior work, and improve your talents and skills. The task of *holding on* to your career includes preserving present career status and achievements while experiencing (or at least perceiving) competition from younger workers. The final task, *reduction of career activities,* includes pre-retirement planning, work reduction or changes, and retirement.

Tips for Self-Assessment

- In what stage of career development am I now?
- If I have not yet reached the *establishment stage,* how might I use the developmental tasks in the *exploration stage?*
- To what extent have I accomplished the career development tasks Super and Jordaan propose?
- Which stage most accurately describes what I want and where I am going?

TABLE 2–1   **Sequence of life stages and career development tasks**

Stages	Career Development Tasks	Approximate Age Range
Exploration	Crystallizing a career preference	14–18
	Specifying a career preference	18–21
	Implementing a career preference	21–24
Establishment	Stabilizing in the chosen career	24–30
	Consolidating career status	30–35
	Advancing in the career	35–44
Maintenance	Holding on to accomplishments and career role	44–64
Decline	Reducing career activities and changes in career-related activities	64 on

SOURCE: Adapted from Super and Jordaan, "Career Development Theory."

Specific behaviors and attitudes are necessary to achieve each of the tasks. Achieving these tasks has a bearing on a person's career maturity—that is, his or her accomplishment of career developmental steps as compared with other individuals of the same age. In examining the career maturity of mid-life adults, Super identifies five factors or basic dimensions; planfulness or time perspective, exploration, information, decision-making, and reality orientation.[4] Super has concluded that tasks, topics to be explored, and kinds of information required of forty year olds are different from those required of adolescents, although the five factors are the same for both groups.

Super states, "Although the content of decision differs, decision-making principles are the same at any age and in dealing with any life stage. Reality orientation may be expected to differ because the mature adult deals with a much greater store of self and work history data, and the external realities relevant to an adult are more clearly defined."[5]

Furthermore, and in conclusion, Super believes earlier career roles affect later ones. He says

> The nonoccupational positions occupied before the adult career begins influence both the adult positions which may be occupied and the way in which their role expectations are met. Thus the amount and type of schooling is one determinant of occupation entered, and the first occupational position, both its type and job performance, is one determinant of later occupational positions open to the individual.[6]

The career to which you are attracted or what you really want to be is your *ideal career self-concept,* but you may sense that something about yourself (your *real career self-concept*) or something within the environment prevents you from attaining your ideal self; therefore, you may consider less desirable options still open. You must explore various careers and define your real career self-concept before you can become the kind of person you desire.

When the kinds of work experiences you face are equivalent to the mental image you hold, you will be satisfied with work and life in general. Hopefully you will discover outlets to exercise your abilities, values, personality traits, and interests.

On the other hand, if your chosen career does not suit your mental image, you may become dissatisfied. You may seek another career where you can fulfill your desired career-role. Some individuals are satisfied with routines. Others prefer creative work, opportunities to express their abilities

[4] Donald E. Super, "A Life-Span, Life Space Approach to Career Development," *Journal of Vocational Behavior,* 16 (November, 1980): 288–298.

[5] Donald E. Super, "Vocational Maturity in Mid-Life Career," *Vocational Guidance Quarterly,* 25 (December, 1977): 295–296.

[6] Super, "A Life-Span, Life Space Approach," 286.

and values. Generally, people are attracted toward a particular career based on their character, behavioral style, and other factors in their background.

PERSONAL ORIENTATION

John L. Holland[7] believes people demonstrate their personal orientation (generally referred to as a personality type) in the selection of a career. He feels each person has stereotypes or certain perceptions of various careers which are emotionally and socially important to that person. Many members of a given profession have similar personal characteristics and react to problems in a similar manner. A person's most frequently expressed personal orientation is the way in which she responds to her work environment. Personal orientations are grouped under the following six descriptions: realistic, investigative, social, conventional, enterprising, and artistic.

A person with a *realistic* personal orientation is likely to work with objects, animals, tools, or technical equipment and avoid social and educational settings. This person feels good about participating in mechanical and athletic activities but does not feel skillful in social ones. On the other hand, the person with an *enterprising* orientation prefers involvement with others, enjoys leadership roles, possesses good verbal skills, and demonstrates persuasive, aggressive, even adventurous traits. Everyone has a combination of orientations, with one dominating his character. For instance, one person's pattern of orientations (ranking from lowest to highest) may be social, enterprising, and conventional.

Tips for Self-Assessment

- **What is my personal orientation? How has it helped my career selection?**
- **Who or what influenced my personal orientation?**
- **What is the relationship of my dominant personal orientation to at least two other less dominant personal orientations?**

Holland believes individuals search for work environments which allow them to express their personal orientations—that is, exercise abilities and skills, express attitudes and values, and deal with agreeable problems and rules while avoiding disagreeable ones. In Table 2–2, Holland labels work environments to correspond with the six personal orientations. An individual having a social personal orientation would function best, for example, in a social work environment. A person's choice of and satisfaction from a career rests largely on whether there is high agreement between

[7]John L. Holland, *Making Vocational Choices: A Theory of Careers,* 2nd ed. (Englewood Cliffs, NJ: Prentice-Hall, 1985).

TABLE 2-2   Personal orientations and related work environments

Themes	Personal Orientations	Work Environments
Realistic	Values concrete and physical tasks; perceives self as having mechanical skills and lacking social skills.	Setting involves concrete, physical tasks requiring mechanical skills, persistence, and physical movement. Careers include machine operator, aircraft mechanic, truck driver, service station worker, draftsperson, barber, and bricklayer.
Investigative	Wants to solve intellectual, scientific, and mathematical problems. Sees self as scholarly, analytical, critical, curious, introspective, and methodical.	Typical settings are research laboratory, diagnostic medical case conference, work group of scientists or medical researchers. Careers include marine biologist, computer programmer, clinical psychologist, architect, dentist, mathematician, and physical scientist.
Artistic	Prefers unsystematic tasks or artistic projects in the form of painting, writing, or drama. Perceives self as imaginative, expressive, original, independent.	Setting involves theater, concert hall, library, radio or television studios. Careers include painter, sculptor, actor or actress, designer, musician, music teacher, symphony conductor, author, editor, reviewer, and radio or television announcer.
Social	Prefers educational, helping, and religious careers. Enjoys such activities as social involvement, church, music, reading, and dramatics. Perceives self as having understanding, liking to help others, and having teaching ability. Values social or ethical activities and is cooperative, friendly, helpful, insightful, persuasive, responsible, and sociable.	Typical settings are school and college classrooms, psychiatrist's office, religious meetings, mental institutions, community and recreational centers. Careers are counselor, nurse, teacher, social worker, judge, missionary, minister, and sociologist.
Enterprising	Values political and economic achievements, supervision, and leadership. Enjoys activities that satisfy personal need for control, verbal expression, recognition, and power. Perceives self as extroverted, sociable, happy, assertive, popular, self-confident, having leadership and persuasive abilities.	Setting involves courtroom, political rally, new car sales room, real-estate firm, and advertising company. Careers include realtor, politician, attorney, professional orator, salesperson, manager.
Conventional	Prefers orderly, systematic, concrete tasks involving verbal and mathematic data. Sees self as orderly, conformist, and having clerical and numerical skills.	Setting involves financial institution (bank), accounting firm, post office, file room, business office, and Internal Revenue office. Careers include banker, accountant, tax expert, timekeeper, financial counselor, key punch operator, secretary, and receptionist.

SOURCE: Adapted from Holland, *Making Vocational Choices*, 19–23, 36–40.

that person's orientation and the work environment. The closer the agreement, the greater the chance for career attainment, career satisfaction, and personal stability.

Tips for Self-Assessment

- What traits do I like (dislike) about my personal orientation?
- What work environment corresponds to my personal orientation?
- What do I like (dislike) about my corresponding work environment?
- What is the likelihood of my being satisfied with my corresponding work environment?

PERSONAL NEEDS

Robert Hoppock,[8] too, assumes career choice is closely associated with personal needs. He believes you will select a career to satisfy your physical and mental needs. Your career choice is influenced by all your needs, but only in proportion to each need's relative strength. You may not understand why your career is satisfactory (or attractive); however, your needs will direct you toward your career choice.

Tips for Self-Assessment

- What are my personal needs?
- How have my needs shaped my ideas about selecting a career?

To better understand Hoppock's theory of personal need structure, refer to Abraham H. Maslow's theory of *hierarchical needs*.[9] This theory explains how people's needs influence their behavior. Maslow suggests that before high-order needs (the kind of needs that are uniquely human and necessary for career planning) can be met, certain primary or basic needs must be satisfied. Eight basic *hierarchical needs* appear in the order in which they must be satisfied. (See Table 2–3).

The most basic need in Maslow's hierarchy is *survival*—the need for food, water, oxygen, and some breathing room. After you meet your survival needs, you fulfill the need for *security* or protection. Next follows the need for *belonging* and acceptance by a group. After the need for belonging, feelings of *self-worth*, usefulness, and recognition may be fulfilled. A need for *information*, knowledge, skills, and for the meaning of symbols and events follows. After that comes the need to *understand* relationships and processes and to combine knowledge and theories. Following this need comes the *aesthetic* need for beauty, order, and balance in all of life. Finally, after all these lower needs are satisfied, there remains the need for *self-actualization*—the need to be fulfilled, to become more perfect, to more

[8] Robert Hoppock, *Occupational Information*, 4th ed. (New York: McGraw-Hill, 1976).
[9] Abraham H. Maslow, *The Farther Reaches of Human Nature* (New York: Viking Press, 1971).

TABLE 2–3   Maslow's hierarchical needs

Highest Need	8. Self-actualization
Aesthetic Needs	7. Aesthetic
Achievement, Intellectual Needs	6. Understanding 5. Information
Affiliation, Social Needs	4. Esteem, worth, self-respect 3. Belonging
Physical, Organizational Needs	2. Security 1. Survival

SOURCE: Adapted from Maslow, *The Farther Reaches of Human Nature.*

fully use one's abilities and skills. Maslow believes that the greatest portion of your time and energy is directed toward satisfying your most basic yet unsatisfied need. As each need becomes more or less fulfilled, a person concentrates on the next higher need.

Maslow's hierarchy may describe how your needs often influence career decisions. Consider an unemployed, twenty-four year old man who has two children, a critically-ill wife, and mortgage payments on the house he is unable to meet. He may concentrate more on his family's lower-order needs than their higher-order ones. He is likely to choose work which will satisfy his survival needs and be less concerned with self-fulfillment, creativity, or status.

Tips for Self-Assessment

- Do personal needs cause me to ignore other important factors when choosing a career?
- To what degree should I allow my personal needs to guide my career behavior?
- How satisfied am I with the direction my needs are taking me?

According to Hoppock, you begin to make career choices after learning which work activities are gratifying. Based on both satisfying and frustrating experiences you will seek out pleasant work and avoid unpleasant situations. You may have had vicarious career experiences through relatives, neighbors, reading, radio, television, and movies. These informed and even misinformed experiences shape and impel career selection. Moreover, if you can determine whether a career will meet your needs before starting it, you may feel satisfied more quickly. To make this determination ahead of time, you must be knowledgable about careers and yourself. Having both self-knowledge and career knowledge will help you recognize a career that will meet your expectations.

BEYOND YOUR PERSONALITY— FACTORS SHAPING CAREER CHOICE

ACCIDENTAL CAREER CHOICES

Tips for Self-Assessment

- What unplanned event or accident, if any, has occurred in my life?
- If so, how has this event or accident influenced my career behavior and/or career choice?
- To what extent would I allow an unplanned event or accident redirect my present career behavior and/or career choice?

Many individuals say they chose their career by accident or as the result of chance. They did not deliberately plan a certain career. They experienced accidents or unforeseeable events such as winning the New York State Lottery or inheriting a business.

SOCIAL FACTORS

Tips for Self-Assessment

- In what ways has my geographical location (city, state, or nation) influenced my career selection?
- How have my education, income, and ethnic group influenced my career choice?

Local, national, and even international surroundings influence your career choices. The opinion of friends, neighbors, and other acquaintances can also sharpen or weaken your focus on a particular career. Social class identification most strongly influences your career choice. Your social position greatly affects your ratings of careers. Major social groups in America perceive certain careers as having prestige or status.

All the preceding social factors—social class membership, perception of role, local/national surroundings, family and educational background, and significant others—influence career choice. Your social class membership includes such parameters as education, income, place and condition of residence, and ethnic group affiliations. How you perceive your career role (for instance, being a leader or follower) shapes your career choice. Common career fields, values, and work opportunities existing within your community also influence your selection. At the same time, you may select a career which is similar to that of a parent or select, for various reasons, a higher-level career than the one a parent holds. The influence of family aspirations on your career selection may vary during your lifetime. Another influence from your family background is the economic conditions you experienced.

Strix Pix

Some people find satisfaction working alone.

For example, you might choose a career if it provides you with an income which permits you to have a lifestyle comparable to your family's. In some circumstances you may avoid layoffs, low pay, unemployment, or under-employment that family members had encountered by choosing a career providing security and/or high income.

High school and college curricula influence a student's career field. Many students enter college with clear ideas about their intended fields of study; whereas, others enter undecided about a specific career. The general courses students often take during their first and second years sometimes help them select a curricular interest consistent with their career goals. It is not uncommon for students who had firm commitments to a curricular program to later change to a completely different program.

Other persons who you consider important (a teacher, counselor, neighbor, employer) may also have some influence on the type of career you

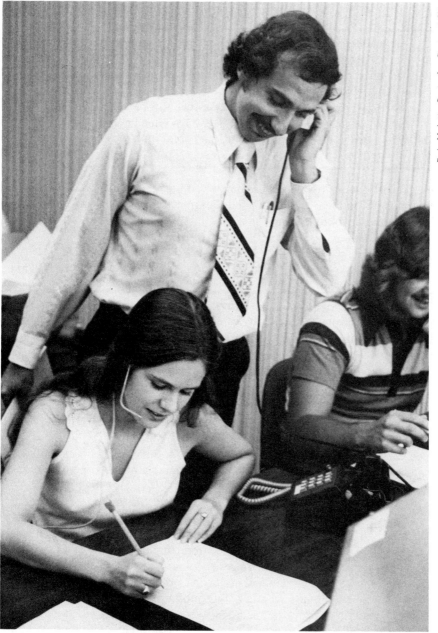

Some find a great deal of pleasure in working with others.

29

OUACHITA TECHNICAL COLLEGE

Tips for Self-Assessment

- What person has had the greatest influence on my preferred career choice?
- What characteristics about this person seemed most impelling?
- How would I evaluate the influence of this person?
- What characteristics do I already have which might be a better guide toward choosing my career than those of another person?

choose. Although this influence may be either positive or negative, it often happens through a student's identification with adults and from adult support and encouragement.

SEX

Tips for Self-Assessment

- To what degree am I allowing my sex and/or traditional expectations to direct my career choice?
- How realistic is using traditional expectations to choose a career?
- Am I allowing sex discrimination to limit my career behavior or career choice?
- How conscious am I of succeeding in my career?
- How hard am I willing to work to attain a successful career?

Recent studies suggest that male and female differences do indeed affect career choice. These differences often occur because women and men approach career choices differently.

Louise Vetter[10] has summarized several factors which influence women's career decisions. Men and women learn early, through career sex-stereotyping, that each may consider only certain career fields. Young males and females, in many instances, have strong stereotypic ways of perceiving traditional sex-linked careers. Personal stereotypic views often restrict the range of careers that women feel are open to them.

Children influence whether their mothers choose to work or choose particular kinds of occupations. Some women with children continue in a career but prefer working in the home so that they can assist their children. Others modify their real or preferred career by reselecting one of less status in order to accommodate the needs of their children. Other mothers manage to fulfill their career-choice needs along with raising their children. How

---

[10]Louise Vetter, "Career Counseling for Women," in *Counseling Women*, ed. L. W. Harmon et al., (Monterey, CA: Brooks/Cole, 1978), 75–93.

women have been socialized shapes their thoughts about and efforts to enter various fields.

Children influence their father's choices too. More men are working at home as *househusbands*—men who take care of home and children while their wife is at work. Suzanne Model's survey[11] revealed that many men are spending more time on housework now that their wives are in the labor force and are unable to spend as much time on household chores. Some studies, such as the one completed by Julia Ericksen and her colleagues,[12] indicate that husbands in blue-collar homes perform more housework than husbands in white-collar homes; however, other studies like William Beer's[13] suggest that the higher a man's career status, the more likely he is to do home chores. One explanation for this later finding is that the greater time-flexibility of professional workers accounts for their ability to mesh career and home requirements.

Another factor which influences women is their conscious or unconscious desire to avoid career success. Often they avoid becoming successful when competing against men. Many settle for less preferred careers because they believe their success may cause them to lose their femininity and their self-concept.

Women's anticipation of sex discrimination in certain fields and the marketplace itself frequently encourages them to subordinate their career interests. A woman may feel that to struggle against sex discrimination on the job is not worth her efforts, considering the likely outcome. In spite of discrimination, many career women are making it in the work world. Expectations about women and careers are changing.

There is no doubt that men face fewer restrictions in their career choices than do women. Generally, society expects and encourages men to achieve vocationally. On the other hand, society expects women to consider sex discrimination, children, expectations of significant others, and fear of career achievement while selecting a career. These factors often restrict or limit women's behavior.

INDECISIVENESS

As high as 50 to 60 percent of entering college students change their major after choosing a different career field.[14] For many reasons college students find it difficult to make a choice. Some commit themselves to unrealistic or uninteresting fields because of parental or societal expectations. They make their career choices without first exploring their values, needs, and abilities.

[11]Suzanne Model, "Housework by Husbands: Determinants and Implications," *Journal of Family Issues,* 2 (October, 1981): 225–237.

[12]Julia A. Ericksen, William L. Yancey and Eugene P. Ericksen, "The Division of Family Roles," *Journal of Marriage and the Family,* 41 (1979): 301–313.

[13]William R. Beer, *Househusbands: Men and Housework in American Families* (New York: J.F. Bergin/Praeger, 1983).

[14]Helen W. Gilbart, *Pathways: A Guide to Reading and Study Skills,* (Boston, MA: Houghton Mifflin Co., 1982), 7.

Tips for Self-Assessment

- Am I ready to commit myself to a career choice?
- How should I go about making my choice?

Choosing prematurely, these students give in to the social pressures of others. Other students are unable to decide on a career because of their inner fears or conflicts. Many are indecisive, unwilling to narrow down their choice to a specific line of work.

Late adolescence is frequently when you choose or commit yourself to a certain career. This choice might suddenly change; at the same time, it is important, since it may influence your lifestyle and behavior over a long period.

CAREER MATURITY

Tips for Self-Assessment

- How have my values shaped my attitude toward a specific career?
- Are my attitudes about this career choice mature?
- Is my career choice realistic?
- Is it consistent with my attitudes, as well as my interests and lifestyle?

In order to make realistic decisions about your future, you need to have developed mature attitudes and competent skills. While many believe selecting one's life work is a matter of chance, this selection may be shaped by a person's degree of career maturity.

Selecting a career is a process which extends over a number of years, beginning during late childhood and continuing into adulthood. The maturity of your attitudes in making a career choice hinges on how consistent your career choices are over a particular period. Another factor you might consider is how realistic is your choice in relation to your abilities, skills, interests, lifestyle, and available work. If you choose to become a fashion designer, interior decorator, or artist but are color-blind, your choice will probably be unrealistic. Another example of an unrealistic choice would be your wanting to become a symphony orchestra conductor when you lack great musical abilities. Preparing for a career as a school counselor when many school systems are reducing their counseling positions makes little sense, regardless of your long desire to entire this field.

Your attitudes and values shape your career plans. They capture and define much of your experience. Attitudes and values can sum up your personal background and learnings, as well as provide you with a unique understanding of individual differences. Values are the element underlying your attitudes which direct your behavior toward certain career goals.

Tips for Self-Assessment

- Upon what basis am I making my career choice?
- Am I considering accurate information about myself, my career choice, and the marketplace as I make my choice?
- Am I making my choice independent of what others think?

John O. Crites[15] identifies five general dimensions which measure career maturity. They are involvement in the choice process, orientation toward work, independence in decision-making, preference for career choice factors, and conceptions of the choice process.

The first dimension deals with the degree to which you actively engage in career selection. Someone might say, "I frequently think about the career I want to have." The second dimension is concerned with whether you have task- or pleasure-oriented attitudes toward work and whether you value work. Examples of this dimension would be, "Work is a beneficial experience," or "I get little satisfaction from working. It's so boring." The third dimension centers on how independent you are in making your career choice. For example, "I intend to choose a career that is similar to the careers of my friends." The third dimension theorizes that if you make a career decision independent of others, your choice will reflect a mature attitude. The fourth decision describes the extent to which you make a career choice based on a specific factor relevant to the choice. A young person might say "I made my choice because I think my skills and education satisfy the requirements for this career." Or, "Sue wants to be an executive secretary because she can earn a high salary." Choosing a career without considering your personal characteristics and pertinent career information can mean your reasoning has been immature. The final dimension is concerned with the accuracy of your understandings in making a career choice. For instance, you might hear a friend say, "I know I can become an accountant. All I need to do is study a lot." Obviously, this is an immature perception of what abilities are necessary in accounting. Mature individuals make career choices after considering educational and work requirements as well as personal characteristics. A detailed discussion in Chapter 5 will help you consider the necessary factors in making a career choice.

A final measure of the maturity of your career choice is the depth of your ability to understand and apply information about specific careers. You should be able to honestly evaluate your strengths and weaknesses in relation to specific career choices. Evaluation will enable you to determine whether or not you are suited for certain kinds of work. If you desire a

[15]John O. Crites, *Theory and Research Handbook CMI* (Monterey, CA: CTB/McGraw-Hill, 1973), 4.

career as a copy editor, for instance, you should know whether or not you have a good knowledge of punctuation, spelling, and grammar. In that particular job, the ability to work with words is all-important. Your ability to look ahead and plan for the career of your choice also indicates your maturity level. Hasty choices may lead to wasted time and career dissatisfaction. Another indicator of career maturity is how well you deal with career-related problems.

In conclusion, your attitudes toward choosing a career, information about yourself and careers, and your planning skills are the best estimates of your career maturity level. Attitudes, information, and planning influence your behavior. Your level of maturity may indicate how you go about deciding your career. A middle-aged adult may have worked for many years, but how well he plans for a career change or how well he understands himself reflect his career maturity. The young adult demonstrates her career maturity by making her decisions independent of others' aspirations. During either adolescence or midlife, your decisions reflect the kinds of experiences you have encountered. You can decide upon your future on the basis of too little, or perhaps too much, information about yourself and career opportunities. Yet, to make a sound decision, consider all the factors.

POINTS TO REVIEW

1. Changes within the career marketplace require that you consider more than a single career choice during the course of your life.
2. Various factors influence career choices.
3. Many adults fail to recognize how they chose their preferred career.
4. It may be beneficial to consider those factors which influence your career choice.
5. Choosing your career independent of others' opinions is likely to lead to improved career satisfaction.
6. Your selection of a career reflects your self-concept.
7. Your character encourages you to seek out those career fields where you can express your personal orientation.
8. Early parent-child interactions can, in part, lead to selections of career categories. (This belief is limited because it ignores other factors contributing to career selection.)
9. Usually, your selected career activities relate to your personal needs. You choose career activities that will satisfy physical and mental needs.
10. Not all career choices are planned. You may accidently find yourself in a particular career that you did not intend as your eventual life's work.
11. Social-class membership, perception of role, local community, family background, educational institutions, and people you consider important influence your career choice. These factors can limit the types of

careers women and men choose, although this trend has begun to change in recent years.

12. Your lack of choice can determine the direction of your career behavior. Indecisiveness may emerge from limited or excessive information about the career world.

13. Your attitudes toward certain fields determine how you decide upon a career. Effective career choice attitudes require you to know yourself and the career world.

14. One measure of a mature career attitude is how independent you are of other individuals when making your career choice. Career maturity can also be measured by how you deal with a set of career concerns compared with other persons of your age. Career concerns during early young adulthood can vary from those encountered in middle age.

Experiential Exercises

1. According to Donald Super, a person's career choice exemplifies her self-image. How would you describe yourself?

2. How has your self-concept influenced your career choice?

3. How might your self-concept influence your career in the future?

4. John Holland has described six personal orientations:

realistic	conventional
investigative	enterprising
social	artistic

   a. Which personal orientation(s) best describes you? (You may choose more than one orientation.)

   b. List characteristics which describe yourself. Does your list suggest that you possess one or more of John Holland's personal orientations, as you indicated in part a ?

c. List one of John Holland's six work environments which might correspond with each of the following careers:

Career	Work Environment
Attorney	
Social worker	
Fashion designer	
Lathe operator	
Accountant	
Microbiologist	
Computer programmer	
Plumber	
Basketball player	
U.S. Senator	
Taxi driver	
Language translator	

5. Robert Hoppock believes your needs influence your career choice. List the psychological needs that your career would have to satisfy.

6. Many persons find themselves in a career as a result of certain unplanned events or accidents. You may have had some type of work experiences in the past and/or present. Which of these work experiences would you describe as unplanned or accidental? Explain.

7. Many factors often influence career choice. Rate the degree of influence of each factor on your career choice in the following chart:

Influencing Factors	Degree of Influence			
	Very Strong	Moderate	Little	None
Your attitude				
Your sex				
Friends				
Significant others (relatives, male or female; friends; husband or wife)				
Community				
Family background				
Education				
Teachers				
Counselors				
Lifestyle				
Indecisiveness				
Interests				

a. Look back over the influence rating chart. Which factor(s) had the greatest amount of influence on your career choice(s) in the past? Explain.

b. Which factor(s) seem to have the greatest influence on the career choice(s) you are presently considering? Explain.

c. What are some possible courses of action you can take to have more influence over your career choice(s)?

8. Describe how the maturity of your career choice has changed according to the following time line.

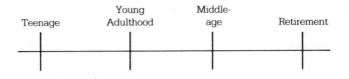

CHAPTER

Achievement rarely occurs without preparation—it requires
forethought and planning.

3

Decision Making

After recognizing that many factors influence your career behavior, you
need to examine the steps involved in making sound, effective decisions.
This process is not always easy, since you may consider many alternatives
before adopting a systematic career plan.

Often, adults must make decisions about significant events. Should I
join a branch of the military service or go to college? What career should I
choose? Am I good enough to succeed in my chosen career? How many
years do I have left to attain my ideal career? As a divorced woman with
one child, how can I obtain solid credentials before I explore the labor
market? Will I be able to locate a career once I finish my college program?
Many adults make decisions only after listening to parents, relatives
counselors, and friends. A few mature adults make their career decisions
independently. Regardless of how or with whom decisions are made,
decision making is a skill which many adults can improve.

Because students invest in many years to attain an education, they
need to plan in order to achieve maximum value from their investment.
Frequently, however, students enter college lacking well-defined career
and educational goals. Perhaps a few students have well-defined goals, but

their steps to attain them are vague, ill-considered. Many adults lack the skills to evaluate options or are unaware of possible alternatives. These shortcomings contribute to unsound decision making in career planning.

This chapter will describe steps involved in career decision making, including the topics of goal building, factors blocking goal setting, avoiding blocks, and setting effective goals. Other important aspects of decision making are linked to knowing your mental and/or physical abilities and surroundings and being willing to take responsibility for your career choice.

FACTORS INFLUENCING DECISIONS

You will not make effective decisions in isolation, without considering other factors. Only in relation to your self-understanding and knowledge of your environment will you make sound choices. The strength of your judgments depends, in part, on how well you apply your knowledge before the moment of decision. Equally important in making effective decisions is the willingness to accept responsibility for your choices.

Tips for Self-Assessment

- **What do I know about myself?**
- **Although I have a career in mind, do my physical and mental abilities fit this choice?**
- **What other career options may more realistically reflect my abilities?**

SELF-KNOWLEDGE

Self-knowledge begins with asking questions such as: What is my career goal? How can I accomplish this goal? How did I decide on the goal(s) I have set for myself? Some people establish educational and career goals beyond their abilities, while others achieve far beyond their expectations. Discrepancies may exist between your ideal career choice and your appraisal of your abilities. In such a case, you may not be realistic about yourself or your choice.

Self-concept, sometimes referred to as self-perception, shapes *how* you make decisions and *what* you decide. As you gain self-knowledge, your self-concept changes. (Obviously the many experiences you acquire during a lifetime influence your self-concept.) When your self-perception is realistic, you can make sound choices. You will easily accept suggestions and will withstand criticism because your assessment of circumstances is accurate.

A realistic self-concept can be an even more powerful tool if you also have knowledge of your aptitudes. *Aptitude* is the ability to learn or understand. Some authorities claim that aptitudes are natural skills or talents. Aptitudes may be manual or mental. Manual aptitudes are identified with a

© Bob Taylor

Self-knowledge begins with asking yourself tough questions.

person's physical activities. Such activities may become skills. Mental aptitudes are associated with intellectual activities. Manual and mental skills influence intelligence and ability. Many careers require both mental and manual aptitude. For instance, Joan, an engineer, needs manual skills to perform her work; she needs mental ones to learn new technology in her profession.

Manual aptitude   Can you easily learn to perform muscular, manipulative, or physical tasks? These aptitudes become critical to a career that requires specific manual skills. The degree of aptitude necessary for success increases as required manual skills increase. Different manual aptitudes are physical dexterity, coordination, muscular rhythm, manual strength, speed of physical movement, and accuracy of movement.

Physical dexterity means the capacity to physically manipulate objects or use the muscles to perform any particular kind of work. The greater the dexterity, the higher the capacity to do complex or difficult physical movements. Certain workers such as surgeons, watchmakers, tool-and-die makers, mechanical trade workers, and welders need dexterity in their hands and fingers to perform their tasks. Others, such as professional athletes, dancers, and heavy equipment operators need overall physical dexterity.

Coordination describes the harmonious adjustment or control of muscles. It involves the use of more than one set of muscles operating simultaneously to produce a successful activity. For example, muscles function simultaneously as you drive your car or walk along the basketball court dribbling a basketball. These activities involve the hands, fingers, arms, eyes, legs, and feet. Eye-hand coordination is a significant aptitude for pianists, artists, watchmakers, architects, keypunch operators, baseball players, and surveyors.

Muscular rhythm is referred to as the physical ability of the human muscular structure to function smoothly. Muscular rhythm helps the timing which is important in various physical activities. Examples of workers who depend on muscular rhythm in their careers are dancers, musicians, and professional athletes.

Manual strength, another physical aptitude, means applying your hand muscles. Manual strength is the potential power that one can physically apply to a given task. Necessary for any career which requires workers to apply physical strength or use manual power, this aptitude is essential in such athletic careers as football, wrestling, and boxing, and also essential in such careers as construction, mining, and freight handling.

Rapidity or speed of physical movement demonstrates the rate of speed at which motor organs can move. For instance, rapidity in arm or finger movement may be useful to a trumpet player, or visual quickness may benefit a linotype operator. Your reaction time, the amount of time you require to recognize a particular stimulus and react to it, is another important factor in rapid physical movement. Your reaction time indicates the quickness with which your muscles work in various situations. Quick, accurate reactions are necessary for the jet pilot, bank teller, professional boxer, air controller, or for anyone who operates a machine or drives a vehicle.

Accuracy of physical movement involves precision or exactness. This exactness is critical for workers such as painters, brain surgeons, crane operators, astronauts, or nurses.

You must consider your physical aptitudes to make sound career decisions. For example, you would not want to attend a teacher education program for four years only to find you could not tolerate standing for seven or more hours a day. Extended periods of standing (or sitting) can be physically demanding.

Mental Aptitude   Essential to problem solving or decision making, all mental tasks require some form of intellectual ability, although standards for mental aptitude differ from one occupation to the next. Understanding your mental aptitude will help you to make sound career and/or educational decisions.

Mental aptitude also involves your ability to reason. Examples of mental aptitudes are verbal reasoning, spatial relationships, mathematical reasoning, mechanical comprehension, auditory discrimination, ability to understand and apply ideas, memory, reasoning, artistic aptitude, and concentration.

Verbal reasoning is the ability to understand both oral and written ideas. The ability to handle verbal symbols and identify relationships is essential in verbal reasoning. The greater the knowledge needed for a career, the higher the degree of verbal reasoning required.

Using spatial relationships or spatial perceptions includes the ability to visualize objects or forms (shapes, sizes, features). One example is the ability to visualize a structure after reading an architectural design. Engineers, architects, computer programers, city planners, and repair or construction workers need this ability.

Mathematical reasoning is the ability to deal with numbers. This reasoning requires that a person identify associations between numerical symbols, as demonstrated in understanding and applying mathematical formulas. Workers who deal in statistics, atomic research, engineering, chemistry, aerodynamics, and physics use mathematical reasoning.

Mechanical comprehension means understanding motion and movement. This ability involves applying mechanical principles as well as understanding and solving mechanical problems. Mechanical engineering and designing, aerodynamics, and astronomy are careers which require mechanical comprehension.

Auditory discrimination is the ability to distinguish different sounds. This ability is essential to an orchestra conductor, a musician, an opera singer, a piano tuner, an automobile mechanic, a recording engineer, and many others.

The ability to understand and apply ideas entails demonstrating mental alertness, determining the importance of ideas, developing ideas for dealing with new experiences, or using basic knowledge to solve problems. You must be capable of receiving verbal instructions and applying them appropriately. College students having top grades often demonstrate their intelligence in the classroom. All formal education and most careers require you to understand and apply ideas.

Memory requires you to recall information and events to which you have been exposed. Necessary in all careers, memory is particularly important for the actor, politician, lecturer, and historian.

Reasoning, the ability to make sound judgments, is used to assemble information from various sources, understand relationships, and establish new patterns. Reasoning ability is required in the legal, science, and mental health professions.

Artistic mental aptitude, the ability to understand and interpret visual responses, is the key to success for designers, artists, and decorators.

Concentration is the ability to resist distraction while focusing on an idea or activity. Some situations require workers to concentrate on one thing at a time; whereas, other jobs may require workers to focus on several areas simultaneously. An editor, for instance, must concentrate in order not to miss a grammatical or technical error. A chef must focus her attention on several areas simultaneously to prepare a full-course meal.

Tips for Self-Assessment

- How much information do I have about the work environment of a particular position?
- What do I know about the functions, responsibilities, and pay of the position?
- How willing am I to assume the responsibilities after accepting the position?

INFORMATION ABOUT SURROUNDINGS

Having accurate information about the social and physical surroundings *(work environment)* of a career helps you reach your stated goals. Your knowledge of surroundings includes facts about other individuals and specific details associated with a career. To obtain knowledge of work surroundings, gather facts from such sources as friends, neighbors, city and state agencies, colleges or universities, newspapers, books, pamphlets, catalogs, and your own perceptions. The greater the amount and quality of information you gather, the greater will be your understanding and awareness of your options.

Consider John, a veterinary student at Oklahoma State University. He wants part-time employment which will give him work experience in veterinary medicine. A friend tells him about the university veterinary medical school hospital's need for an animal-care keeper in one of its laboratories. The hospital needs to fill this job within two or three weeks, after the student who presently cares for the animals graduates.

John goes to the hospital having some questions in mind: How will I get to and from the lab since I don't own a car? How long will I be expected to work each day? How many days of the week will I be expected to work? What is the pay for this position? What tasks will I be required to perform?

While at the hospital lab, John talks with one of his professors who tells him about a part-time position as a graduate medical assistant to Professor Smith. John also talks with the student who will be vacating the animal-care position to find out more about his responsibilities.

At this point John has several options. He can work as an animal-care keeper, Monday through Sunday, 9 A.M. to 1 P.M., feeding and grooming small animals, gaining medical experience. He will have to ride his bicycle six blocks to the lab and will earn $150 every two weeks. He can work as a

Essential to decision making is taking responsibility for your choices.

graduate medical assistant to one of the veterinary professors at the hospital, working three hours each day, Monday through Friday. In this position he will assist Professor Smith in animal care and gather veterinary information through library search. He will ride his bicycle six blocks to the lab and can earn $195 every two weeks. He can volunteer with a local veterinarian, gaining some medical experience. He will volunteer once a week for two and a half hours, ride the bus for twenty-five minutes to the veterinarian's office, but receive no pay.

Because John has collected information, he can make an informed decision. By collecting the information, he has increased his options.

TAKING RESPONSIBILITY

Essential to any decision you make is taking responsibility for it. You must willingly accept the consequences resulting from your choice. Some authorities[1] in the field of career decision making claim that the extent to which

---

[1]H. B. Gelatt et al., *Decisions and Outcomes* (New York: College Entrance Examination Board, 1973), 32.

you demonstrate responsibility in the decision process indicates career maturity or lack of it.

Another consideration related to taking responsibility is commitment to a stated goal and the amount of effort put forth to attain it. Your willingness to decide about present events limits the opportunities which might be available to you in the future. The degree to which you are willing to make a choice is called *decisiveness*. Decisiveness, the willingness to carry out decisions, reflects your responsibility and commitment.

The three components—self-knowledge, knowledge of environment, and responsibility—are, indeed, crucial to effective decision making. If you have objective self-knowledge, know or have explored your environment, and assume responsibility for your choices, you are likely to make a sound decision.

SETTING GOALS

A *goal* can be defined as a purpose, an aim, or an objective in your life that you aspire to attain. In any decision-making situation, it is important for you to have a purpose. As you set personal goals for yourself, you will find this process frees you from frustration and worry. Furthermore, you will make fewer decisions dependent on situational factors (spur-of-the-moment decisions).

Tips for Self-Assessment

- To what extent do I recognize a need to set a personal career goal?
- If not, what is going on in my own thinking that would be preventing my goal setting?
- What can I do to eliminate that which is blocking my goal setting behavior?
- What are some general steps that I can apply in setting career goals for myself?

IRRATIONAL BELIEFS—BLOCKING BEHAVIOR

Often people are able to state goals but face factors which block their willingness to accept or act on their stated goals. If you believe your goals are unimportant, you are less likely to accomplish them. Feelings of guilt and invalid excuses are other blocks against obtaining your goals. Figure 3–1 illustrates setting goals in Examples A and B along with irrational or faulty thinking which prevents acting on your goals.

How many times have you "talked to yourself" about your career and reached these kinds of conclusions? "What's the use of setting goals for myself when I'm forty-two years old? I'm over the hill." "Most of my friends

FIGURE 3–1   Irrational thinking which can block goal attainment

Goals	Blocking Behavior
Example A	
I want to increase my concentration during the career planning workshop —concentrate on the presentation for one and a half hours Mondays, Wednesdays, and Fridays during the spring semester.	1. Gee, the weather is beautiful. It's really hard to pay attention to what Ms. Smith presents.
	2. Career planning is such a boring subject. It's not easy to stay awake during class.
	3. I'm a night person. I don't function well early in the morning, especially on Mondays, Wednesdays, and Fridays.
Example B	
I want to narrow my decision to three career choices in six weeks.	1. It just seems that I don't have time to get to the library.
	2. I have started considering one of my choices, but it takes a lot of time.
	3. I would start on them if I really knew what these career counselors wanted.
	4. I feel so guilty about not spending time with Sue. You know, we are engaged to be married in June. And besides, a lot of times I just don't feel like seriously thinking about some stupid, old career.

have made it without any real career purpose in mind—why should I be different?" "If I set goals for myself now, I'll only have to change them later. Why be bothered with them in the first place?" "Although I'm dissatisfied with my career and would like to try another, the competition in a higher-paying field is too great for me to consider something else." "Now that our children are on their own, there is little need for me to set new goals for myself—my real purpose in life, caring for my children, is now nonexistent." Each of these statements implies, "This goal is not for me," or "I'm not interested in setting goals for myself." Consequently, as you evaluate those thoughts you trigger indifferent or negative feelings toward goal setting. Even though you have the power to continue setting or planning your goals, you do neither.

But suppose you think, "Fantastic! I've been overdue in thinking about some type of career goal for myself—I don't know why I didn't think of this sooner." These statements suggest, "My goals will benefit me." As a result, you evaluate these thoughts positively. Should you really believe them, these thoughts urge you toward goal setting.

FIGURE 3-2   **ABC process for rational career thinking**

A Your Perception	B Your Self-Talk Evaluation	C Your Emotional Consequences
I wasn't hired for the consumer specialist position. Another woman got it."	"This is awful! I really must be a worthless person."	You express anger and/or hostility.
	"Everything happens to me."	You refuse to consider new goals.
	"Those SOBs. How could they do this to me? That's terrible."	You disregard further prospects of attaining a position as a consumer specialist.

Inability or just indifference can influence your decision to formulate career goals for the present and future. You should realize that irrational or faulty beliefs often block goal-setting behavior. It is not the event itself, but rather your interpretation of that event which causes your emotional reaction. Consequently you refuse to state your career goals. Note the following ABC example.

Figure 3-2 shows a chain reaction occurs once you encounter certain experiences.[2] Section A presents your actual perception of an event. Section B describes your interpretation or self-talk about this event. Section C shows what you would do as a result of your irrational or faulty beliefs shown in Section B. This sequence only describes your *complete feelings,* your feelings as they are when you first learn them. The important word here is *habit.* When you habitually think the same positive, negative, or neutral thoughts, occurring in B, about similar specific perceptions of external events, occuring in A, you will begin to get the same type of positive, negative, or neutral self-talk about those perceptions. Regardless of how your self-talk or interpretations get started, you can still change them by changing your conscious thoughts and their implied attitudes and beliefs. Your sincere thoughts indicate your attitudes and beliefs.

ELIMINATING BLOCKING BEHAVIOR

Little, if anything, comes from just thinking. Thoughts only determine how you may act, if at all, on your goals. Developing excellent career goals is insufficient. You must act upon them. An only fair career goal developed and acted upon is 100 percent better than an exciting goal which has died from inaction.

[2]Maxie C. Maultsby, Jr., *Help Yourself to Happiness—Through Rational Self-Counseling* (New York: Institute for Rational Living, Inc., 1975), 27–65.

FIGURE 3-3   ABC process for rational career thinking, continued

D	E
Disputing Faulty Beliefs	Your Emotions and Actions for the Future
"Where is the evidence that because I wasn't hired as the consumer specialist, that I am a worthless person, or that I'm awful."	"It's annoying that another woman got the position, but I don't feel angry or hostile." "Just because I didn't get the position doesn't mean I'm going to stop working toward my career goal."

A stated goal is only as good as your willingness to prevent negative factors from blocking necessary steps for you to accomplish that goal. If you systematically get rid of old habits, self-defeating fears, and anger, you can act upon your goals. To eliminate your faulty self-talk occurring in Section B, as well as negative feelings and inactivity in Section C, you need to consider more steps in Sections D and E. The continuation of the *ABC Process* in Figure 3-3 introduces disputing your faulty thoughts (Section D) and new emotional consequences (Section E).

Disputing faulty thoughts involves re-examining the initial facts and events as well as re-evaluating your thoughts about them.[3] While re-examining your perceptions, you need to think, "If I had to take a snapshot of what I said had happened, would I see more or less than what I'm considering as the facts?" Or, "How much of what I see and hear now is fact compared to what I had said happened earlier?" The second step requires that you determine if your thoughts are based on facts rather than opinions. You learn to base your thoughts on facts first and opinions second, if at all. Section E is designed to help you formulate emotional goals for the future. This requires your describing the emotions you want to feel or actions you will take in future situations, rather than the ones you have just experienced. Section E replaces feelings or actions from Section C.

The ABC method can help you set and act upon your career goals. Another method may also prove useful. You can establish career goals by using the following steps.

1. Objectively examine your behavior. Determine what you have to do to eliminate any blocking behavior you experience. Decide what you need to do differently.
2. Interview a person who has eliminated a blocking behavior that seems to be like yours. Determine how this person managed to stop the behavior.
3. Explore as many ideas as you can which might remove blocking behavior to your stated goal.

[3]Ibid., 55–60.

In conclusion, eliminating blocking behavior requires you to take action independent of the problem situation. Thus, it is essential that you become aware of your own blocking behavior in order to take steps to eliminate it.

A person may not easily determine when he has fulfilled an old goal or when he must set a new one. For instance, twenty-eight year old Charles has been out of high school and has worked as an unskilled laborer for the last three years. Recently he has begun to feel dissatisfied because he has been unable to do interesting things with his life. Charles may remain dissatisfied because he has never seriously examined his purpose or considered setting goals necessary to obtain those things he thinks he wants.

Initially, Charles needs to identify the problem—in this case, boredom with his present job. His second step should be considering methods which would solve the problem or improve his present situation. Third, he should narrow his solution to the best one he knows he can realistically implement. Fourth, he should assume his goal can and should be reached. Therefore, he should be able to list ways in which his goal will improve the problem situation. This last step may help Charles set up a list of desired outcomes. Later Charles can refer to his list and indicate whether or not he has accomplished his goal.

PRESENT, SHORT-RANGE, AND LONG-RANGE DECISIONS

Tips for Self-Assessment

- To what degree am I considering only present goals?
- In what way might my present decisions influence my future?

Many adults consider making decisions, whether serious or trivial, an ongoing process which helps them gain control over events in their life. Decisions, however, are somewhat interdependent. Specific decisions concerning the present (Which academic major should I pursue?) depend in part on vague decisions about the future (Which law school should I attend, if I'm accepted? As a lawyer, how would I go about attracting clients?). You should also realize that decisions regarding the future will steadily change as a result of making decisions about the present. Consider Bill, who first decided to be a high school mathematics teacher with a master's degree. However, he changed his undergraduate major to social studies after learning that his grades in political science courses were superior to those in his mathematics courses. Now he is confident that he can pass the bar examination and will be able to afford to attend law school. While your actions are not irreversible, your present judgements will, to some extent, determine later judgments. In conclusion, decisions change in varying degrees as you gain understanding of yourself and your world.

EFFECTIVELY APPLYING DECISION-MAKING SKILLS

As stated earlier, decision making requires assessing and using a set of skills. These skills, your learned behaviors, illustrate ways to solve problems and make decisions. Needs or preferences will dictate your decision-making strategies for reaching goals. Some of us use a single plan, a consistent pattern of decision making, whereas others apply several strategies for each decision. Strategies are based on values, goals, information, and commitment. How you apply these skills determines your decision-making plan.

Tips for Self-Assessment

- How would I describe my style of making decisions?
- To what extent am I aware of this decision-making style?
- Do I apply this style in most situations?
- What are the strengths and weaknesses of my decision-making style?
- How can I improve my style to ensure more effective decisions?

DECISION-MAKING STYLES

For many, decision making is a conscious effort involving feelings, values, attitudes, commitments, perceptions, and available information.[4] On the other hand, others are less aware of what goes on during their decision-making processes. How you resolve problems or make decisions illustrates your style of collecting, processing, and applying information. The way in which you consistently make decisions or solve problems is referred to as a *style*. For example, if you are systematic today, you will not spontaneously reach a decision tomorrow.

Decision-making styles may be grouped into three general categories, each category containing subgroups.[5] The styles of decision-making are shown in Figure 3–4.

DEVELOPING A DECISION-MAKING STYLE

Consider using a planned approach to the decision-making process. Try this four-step procedure.

1. Identify the need to make a decision by clearly stating a goal or purpose. Consider Elaine who begins examining what she wants as a career. She chooses to be an administrative nurse. She has established a long-range goal but is undecided about which college to attend. Therefore,

---

[4]R. H. Johnson, "Individual Styles of Decision Making: A Theoretical Model for Counseling," *Personnel and Guidance Journal* (1978): 530–536.

[5]Anna Miller-Tiedeman and Muriel Tomkins Niemi, "An 'I' Power Primer: Part Two—Structuring Another's Responsibility into His or Her Action," *Focus on Guidance*, 9 (1977): 1–20.

FIGURE 3-4   Decision-making styles

Styles	Examples
1. *Spontaneous*	
a. Impulsive	You react now; think little about it later, if any.
b. Intuitive	You respond immediately to only the first and/or second alternatives without considering others; choices are made according to your hunches, without considering related information.
c. Hopeful	You make your choice solely on what you desire or find the most appealing without considering the relevant facts pertaining to self, surroundings, and the decision situation.
2. *Purposeful*	
a. Planned	You state clear goals for yourself, plan how you intend to achieve them, and work hard in putting your plans into action.
b. Analytical	You are systematic in planning and achieving your goals; before choosing your options, you usually examine all information and experiences in detail to get an overall picture of relevant information, the decision situation, and possible consequences.
c. Open	You select the option that will produce the least amount of negative results; you are open or willing to take a risk in choosing the most promising options available.
d. Complex	You start out with clearly stated goals, examine your decision situation thoroughly, and begin to gather relevant information; however, you become extremely confused with all the information collected, and are unable to reach the point of making a choice.
3. *Deferred*	
a. Reluctant	You are aware that you should be working toward your goal, but you just don't seem to be able to "get with it."
b. Delayed	You know that you should try to gather the information today about the job opening in the dean's office, but you decide to do it another time next week.
c. Aimless	You really don't care how you will meet your goals; you just don't want to deal with them.
d. Predetermined	You are unwilling to make decisions because you feel that external events or factors have control of your life; it is useless to make any decisions.
e. Passive	You feel that it is unnecessary to make decisions because other people will make them for you, so why make any decisions?

Elaine's short-range goal is finding a suitable college which will help pre-pare her for administrative nursing. Although she has considered two colleges in her home state, Elaine is not sure that either of these would be her best option.

2. Gather relevant information about possible alternatives. Elaine should then ask herself: "What is the size of the student population com-pared to the teaching faculty? Does the college award the type of degree I want? What is the cost of attending this college in comparison to attending others? What financial aid programs does the college have? How far away is the college from home? What kind of social life do the students have? What is the quality of the college's curricula or preparation programs? What are the college's admission policies, requirements? What extracurricular activities are provided for students?

To answer these questions, Elaine must start collecting information about in-state and out-of-state colleges other than the two she has already considered. She may examine college catalogs or general guides to colleges. She may write to various colleges to obtain specific information. She may send letters requesting information about financial assistance to private, state, and federal agencies. She may gather information from talks with friends, counselors, teachers, parents, college financial aid officers, and college professors.

3. Use the information gathered to study possible actions and prob-abilities. Based on information Elaine has collected, she should be able to estimate the chances of a college accepting her on the basis of her grade-point averages and test scores. If she realistically evaluates her mental and physical skills, she should be able to estimate her chances of success at each of the colleges she has considered. Most importantly, taking this step will enable Elaine to narrow her options.

4. Apply personal values to the possible options. Elaine must consider what she most values about the colleges which accept her. For instance, Elaine may consider such questions as: "Will my graduation from this college increase my chances of getting a high salary? Is the atmosphere between students and professors friendly, warm? Does the college provide opportunities for students to become involved in extracurricular activities such as drama and sports? Does the college require its students to live on campus, to be in dormitories at certain hours of the night? Does the college permit its students to smoke cigarettes and drink beer on campus? Does the college require women to wear dresses or skirts on campus? Is the campus in an urban or rural setting?"

You must carefully weigh your values in relation to your options by evaluating possible outcomes and eliminating less desirable alternatives. Elaine will re-evaluate the colleges based on her information and her personal values. After evaluating the colleges, she will make judgments about them. Elaine will then eliminate the least desirable college (or alternative). As Elaine evaluates the remaining alternatives, she will con-tinue to eliminate until she reaches a choice. Now Elaine compares the college of her choice to her original goal to determine if the college meets the standards she had set.

Occasionally you may be unable to reach a final selection after the last step of the decision-making process. Suppose that Elaine eliminates five of the least desired colleges among nine possibilities. After spending time re-evaluating the remaining colleges, she finds herself unable to eliminate the last four alternatives. She will need to gather more information about her alternatives. Therefore, she needs to repeat steps one to four.

Decision making is essential to career planning. How well you make decisions will determine how effective you will be in achieving your career goals. Equally important to both decision making and career planning is knowing yourself. Once you have learned to apply the steps involved in decision making, the next step is to explore how careers are classified within the labor market.

POINTS TO REVIEW

1. Both external and internal factors influence your decisions.
2. Factors which influence decision making are personal values, self-concept, interests, mental and physical abilities, personal needs, family and other important persons, risk-taking, educational curriculum, information, and place of residence.
3. Your values help shape your beliefs, which in turn influence your behavior.
4. The way you see yourself often determines your career choices.
5. You should be aware of any differences between your interests and career choices.
6. A goal is referred to as a purpose, aim, or objective in life.
7. The four steps in establishing a goal are to identify the problem, consider methods to solve the problem, objectively narrow the solutions to the best ones, and list ways in which the goal will improve the problem situation.
8. Irrational or faulty beliefs can block your ability to set goals.
9. You can eliminate blocking behavior by objectively examining your behavior, interviewing others who experience blocking behavior, and exploring a variety of ways that may remove such behavior.
10. Considering accurate social and physical information about your surroundings will enable you to attain your career goal.
11. Career decision making requires you to take responsibility for the outcomes of your decision.
12. How you solve problems or make decisions reflects your personal behavioral style.
13. Since you and the career marketplace will change in the future, you will have to make decisions throughout your life.

Experiential Exercises

1. Many factors influence your decisions. These factors are internal (inside you) or external (outside you). The following chart lists both external and internal factors and allows you to rate the degree of influence each factor may have.

   a. Rate the degree of influence each factor has on your decisions by placing a check mark ($\sqrt{}$) in the appropriate space.

Influencing Factors	Degree of Influence				
	Strong	Medium	Low	Slight	None
1. Myself					
2. Parents					
3. Brothers and/or sisters					
4. Husband or wife					
5. Neighbors					
6. Friends of same age					
7. Teachers					
8. Counselors					
9. Community workers					
10. Readings from books, newspapers, and other sources					
11. Television and/or radio					
12. Educational curriculum					
13. Social and economic conditions					
14. Place of residence					

b. Re-examine the factors influencing your decision making. Put another check mark (√) next to those influencing factors which you feel are most important for your decision making. What are the advantages and disadvantages of those factors?

c. How might you become more independent in your future decision making?

2. Before setting goals for yourself, evaluate those aspects of your life which may need to be changed or improved.

   a. List the aspects of your life you would like to change or improve.

   b. In what ways would you like to improve them?

   c. If you were to achieve your goal, in what ways would your life be better?

   d. How would you know that you had achieved your goal?

   e. List behaviors which may block or prevent you from achieving goals.

   f. What plan of action can you use to eliminate these behaviors?

3. Decisions you make during different periods of time may overlap with each other. For instance, what you decide tomorrow may influence decisions you will make in three weeks. These latter decisions may influence your decisions in a year.

   a. List some *present decisions* (to be made now), *short-range decisions* (to be made weeks or months away), and *long-range decisions* (to be made one or more years away).

Present	Short-Range	Long-Range
1.	1.	1.
2.	2.	2.
3.	3.	3.
4.	4.	4.

   b. Describe how your decisions listed in *a.* are related to or dependent on you rather than on others.

4. Knowing who you are is particularly important when you must make decisions. Other than just stating your name and occupation, tell who you are.

   a. Describe yourself. *How* do you see yourself?

b. Try to realistically evaluate yourself by listing your strengths and weaknesses.

Strengths	Weaknesses
1.	1.
2.	2.
3.	3.
4.	4.
5.	5.
6.	6.

c. How do others see you?

d. Are their views different from or similar from your own? Explain.

5. Values may cause you to feel worthwhile, meaningful, or important. They sometimes influence the way you think or act.

a. What kinds of things in your life seem worthwhile? Explain.

b. What kinds of things seem the least important? Explain.

6. It is helpful to determine how your values relate to your career choice. Rate the following value statements by placing a check mark ($\sqrt{}$) in the appropriate boxes.

Career Values	Most Important	Slightly Important	Least Important
1. A career that allows me to create or develop new products and/or ideas.			
2. A career that provides me with the feeling I am doing a task well.			
3. A career that provides me with the security of knowing I will keep it during hard times.			
4. A career that can be performed in pleasant surroundings; away from noisy, cold, hot, or dirty conditions.			
5. A career that allows me to plan and direct other workers' activities.			
6. A career that permits me to work at my own pace and do things which interest me.			
7. A career that pays well and permits me to attain my wants as well as my basic needs.			
8. A career that allows me to work for the welfare of other human beings.			
9. A career setting where management does not favor males or females and various ethnic and cultural groups.			
10. A career that permits me to perform a variety of work activities.			
11. A career that provides me with high status in the eyes of others in my particular field.			
12. A career that allows me to think independently and learn how and why certain things function.			

Re-examine your list to find the most important career values. Place another check mark next to those values which you believe are most important for your career success and satisfaction. What careers are likely to meet the needs of your most important career values? List these careers below.

7. Another part of making sound career decisions is having an understanding of your physical and mental abilities. Rate your abilities in the following exercise by placing a check mark in the appropriate boxes.

Physical Abilities	Self-rating of abilities		
	High	Average	Low
1. Finger dexterity			
2. Muscular coordination			
3. Muscular rhythm			
4. Manual strength			
5. Speed of physical movement			
6. Accuracy of physical movement			

Mental Abilities	Self-rating of abilities			
	Excellent	Very Good	Fair	Poor
1. Verbal reasoning				
2. Spatial perception				
3. Arithmetical reasoning				
4. Mechanical comprehension				
5. Auditory discrimination				
6. Understanding and applying ideas				
7. Memory				
8. Making sound judgments				
9. Concentration				

Re-examine your list of physical and mental abilities. Place a check mark next to the physical abilities you believe are most important for your career success. Next, place a check mark next to the mental abilities that you feel are the best indicators for your career success. List careers which best correspond with your highly-rated physical and mental abilities.

8. Betty will graduate next semester from Westbrook College as a dental hygienist. She has begun sending copies of her resumé to various dentists and dental clinics. Planning to remain in the Westbrook community, Betty is considering career possibilities there. Betty has become interested in an advertisement from one of the local dental clinics to work five days a week as a hygienist for $18,000 a year.

   a. As Betty investigates this career opportunity, what concerns might she have about her surroundings in relation to this career possibility?

   b. What sources of information may help her better understand how her surroundings relate to this position?

9. Taking responsibility in the decision-making process affects the outcomes of the process. The degree of responsibility taken for a situation often determines how well goals might be achieved. Read and respond to the following exercise.

   Bill has completed high school and takes a job as a nursing assistant at Denton General Hospital. After working there for a year and a half, he is laid off and is not called to work in eight months. Bill says that he wants his former job back or any other job that pays well. He lives at home with his mother and father. Yet, since he has been out of work, Bill has hung around the neighborhood corner talking to his friends and shooting pool. When at home, Bill usually sleeps or plays records.

Evaluate Bill's situation. In what ways do you feel that Bill should assume responsibility? What things might be preventing Bill from setting goals and taking some kind of action?

10. To help understand yourself in decision-making situations, identify your decision style. Place check marks in the appropriate boxes to indicate how often you use specific decision styles.

Styles	How often do I use them?				
	Al-ways	Very Often	Often	Some-times	Never
1. Spontaneous					
a. impulsive					
b. intuitive					
c. hopeful					
2. Purposeful					
a. planned					
b. analytical					
c. open					
d. complex					
3. Deferred (or delayed)					
a. reluctant					
b. postponed					
c. aimless					
d. fateful					
e. passive					

11. List the four steps of a planned decision-making process.

1.

2.

3.

4.

12. Helen will graduate from high school next year with a B+ average. She wants to go to the local college but is unable to choose a specific course of study. Helen has been considering accounting or math education as college majors. Describe how you could apply the steps in the decision-making process (question *13*) to Helen's situation.

13. Tim has finished high school and wants to be an engineer. He placed slightly below the top ten percent of the students who took the Scholastic Aptitude Test. Tim comes from a working-class family. He is considering whether to become an engineer by joining the Navy or going to college. Describe how you would apply the decision-making model to Tim's situation.

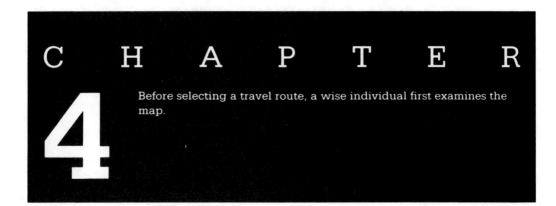

C H A P T E R

4

Before selecting a travel route, a wise individual first examines the map.

Classification of Careers

A sound career plan is incomplete without knowledge of various fields of work. With more than 35,000 different careers in the United States, you would be limiting your choice should you consider only a few possibilities. Ideally, you should have extensive knowledge of all existing careers, but this notion is unrealistic. Various methods of classification currently exist which organize career information.

Career categories enable you to understand the relationships between and among various career groups. Several systems classify careers; however, you should recognize that no classification method is better than another. The needs of a twenty-two year old college student, who is beginning to think about work, are different from those of a fifty-four year old public school teacher, who is concerned about starting a new career after his retirement. Yet, each of them requires information about the marketplace to make sound career decisions.

Tips for Self-Assessment

- What do I know about the many ways in which the labor market is classified?
- Although I have a rough idea about what career I want, how will exploring the classification systems help me make a more informed career choice?
- In what way is one system better for me than another?
- What else can I learn about careers other than the way they are classified?

This chapter explores concepts which undergird the structure of the career market. Surveying several career classification systems will help you improve your decision-making skills, provide you with information about jobs and industries, and reveal characteristics of various careers.

Several systems classify *occupations*, names of similar tasks or work performed in different organizations. This chapter introduces four classification systems—career code; ideas, people, and things; industries; and career families.

CAREER CODE CLASSIFICATIONS

The fourth edition of the *Dictionary of Occupational Titles* (DOT), developed by the U.S. Department of Labor,[1] uses a nine-digit career (or occupational) code (for example, 191.267–010). Together, these nine digits provide an identification code for a particular career which differentiates it from all others.

The first three digits indicate a career group. All careers are organized into nine broad categories represented by the first digit. The first category, professional, technical, and managerial careers, is signified with the first digit being either a zero (0) or a one (1). The other eight categories begin with a first digit from two (2) to nine (9). These broad categories are listed as follows.

0/1	Professional, technical, and managerial careers
2	Clerical and sales careers
3	Service careers
4	Agricultural, fishery, forestry, and related careers
5	Processing careers
6	Machine trade careers
7	Bench work careers
8	Structural work careers
9	Miscellaneous careers

[1]U.S. Department of Labor, *Dictionary of Occupational Titles*, 4th ed. (Washington, DC: U.S. Government Printing Office, 1977).

The *professional, technical, and managerial careers* category includes positions dealing with the theoretical and practical features of such fields as architecture; engineering; mathematics; physical sciences; social sciences; medicine and health; education; museum, library, and archival sciences; law; theology; the arts; recreation; administrative specialties; and management. Additionally, this category describes careers which support scientists and engineers, for example, operating radios, piloting aircraft, and directing the course of ships. Most of the support careers require substantial educational preparation, usually at a university, college, community junior college, or technical institute.

The *clerical and sales careers* category has two subcategories. Clerical careers deal with preparing, transcribing, systematizing, and preserving records, distributing information, and collecting accounts. Sales careers include influencing customers in favor of a commodity or service. Careers closely identified with sales transactions are part of this subcategory, even though they do not entail active involvement in the selling process. Clerical workers usually receive specialized training in high school or college. Educational requirements for sales vary with the career, ranging from no specific requirements for some store clerks to college degrees for salespersons dealing with sophisticated products or services. For many sales positions, high school training, good interpersonal skills, and the ability to convince people are the only requirements.

Service careers deal with providing domestic services in private homes; preparing food and drink in commercial, institutional, or other establishments; providing lodging and related services; providing grooming, cosmetic, and other personal and health care services for children and adults; maintaining and cleaning clothing or other apparel; providing protection for people and property; attending to the comfort or requests of patrons; and cleaning and maintaining building interiors. Many service careers require few special abilities and little, if any, educational training. One can learn most of these careers through experience or on-the-job training. Some personal service careers do require training courses, ranging from a few months to a year.

Agricultural, fishery, forestry, and related careers focus on propagating (or multiplying), growing, caring for, and gathering plant and animal life and products; logging timber tracts; catching, hunting, and trapping animal life; and caring for parks, gardens, and grounds. In addition, there are careers which provide related support services. Some agricultural workers state that job experience best prepares them for work, while others, working in scientific aspects of agriculture, say they must first study techniques and methods at a four-year agricultural college. Many fishery workers learn the business through experience. Forestry requirements vary according to the level of the position.

Processing careers deal with refining, mixing, compounding, chemically treating, heat treating, or similarly working materials and products.

Workers must have a knowledge of relevant processes and follow specific formulas or other requirements. Processing equipment includes mixing machines, crushers, grinders, vats, stills, ovens, or furnaces. Educational preparation requirements vary but can include completing high school, apprenticeship, college, or technical institute. Most skilled workers serve a three- or four-year apprenticeship. Some beginners become journeymen because of educational training and/or work experience.

Machine trade careers include operating machines which feed into or prepare other machines to bore, cut, mill, print, abrade (wear down or scrape away) and similarly handle such materials as stone, paper, wood, and metal. This career category requires some complex tasks. Complex work may be understanding machine functions, reading blueprints, making mathematical calculations, and making decisions to obtain adherence to particulars. Simple tasks may require outstanding eye-hand coordination. These broad tasks include disassembly, repair, reassembly, installation, machinery and mechanical maintenance, weaving, and knitting. Educational requirements vary based on the level of a position within this category. Many entry requirements in machine trade careers are similar to those in the processing careers category.

Bench work careers deal with using hand tools and bench machines to fabricate or repair relatively small items, such as light bulbs, tires, jewelry, or footwear. Generally workers are at a bench, worktable, or conveyor, located in a plant or shop. At more complex levels, a worker must be able to read blueprints, follow patterns, apply various hand tools, and assume responsibility to attain standards. At less complex levels, she might be responsible for following accepted work procedures. Preparation often can be obtained through work apprenticeship, vocational-technical schools, or community college.

The *structural work careers* category focuses on repairing, installing, paving, erecting, and fabricating structures and structural parts. Work usually takes place outside a factory or shop environment, except for factory production line careers. Although workers use stationary machines, the machines are less important than hand tools and power tools. Often, workers must be knowledgeable of the capabilities of their materials in regard to stress, durability, and resistance. This career category requires some skills, although workers can learn them in a relatively short time—a few weeks or months—or while working. Educational requirements may vary according to the functional level of the work performed.

The *miscellaneous careers* category represents careers which deal with transporting persons; packaging and transporting materials; mining; producing and distributing utilities; providing varied services in the communication media; producing graphic work; and working at other unlisted careers. The unskilled work in this category is among the easiest to enter because educational and training requirements may not be very high.

The U.S. Department of Labor further breaks down these nine broad career categories into ninety-seven career divisions and describes them in detail in the DOT *(Dictionary of Occupational Titles)*. Say you want to find information about the career title, real estate appraiser, whose DOT nine-digit code number is 191.267–010. The first digit (1) indicates that this particular career is found in the category, *professional, technical, and managerial careers.*

The second digit indicates the division within the category. There are fifteen divisions within the professional, technical, and managerial careers category. These divisions follow:

00/01	Careers in architecture, engineering, and surveying
02	Careers in mathematics and physical sciences
04	Careers in life sciences
05	Careers in social sciences
07	Careers in medicine and health
09	Careers in education
10	Careers in museum, library, and archival sciences
11	Careers in law and jurisprudence
12	Careers in religion and theology
13	Careers in writing
14	Careers in art
15	Careers in entertainment and recreation
16	Careers in administrative specializations
18	Managers and officials, not elsewhere classified
19	Miscellaneous professional, technical, and managerial careers

In the example, the first two digits (19) locate the career in the miscellaneous professional, technical, and managerial careers division. The third digit combined with the first two (191) defines the career group within the division. The eight groups within the *miscellaneous professional, technical, and managerial careers* division are as follows:

191	Agents and appraisers, not elsewhere classified
193	Radio operators
194	Sound, film, videotape recording, and reproduction careers
195	Careers in social and welfare work
196	Airplane pilots and navigators
197	Ship captains, mates, pilots, and engineers
198	Railroad conductors
199	Miscellaneous professional, technical, and managerial careers

The three digits in the example (191) locate the career in the *Agents and appraisers* career group.

The middle three digits of the DOT classification code describe three tasks the worker performs in a particular career. Every career requires a person to perform, to some degree, in relation to data (ideas), people, and things. Each middle digit indicates the worker's relationship to these factors.

DATA (4th Digit)	PEOPLE (5th Digit)	THINGS (6th Digit)
0 Synthesizing	0 Mentoring	0 Setting Up
1 Coordinating	1 Negotiating	1 Precision Working
2 Analyzing	2 Instructing	2 Operating/Controlling
3 Compiling	3 Supervising	3 Driving/Operating
4 Computing	4 Diverting	4 Manipulating
5 Copying	5 Persuading	5 Tending
6 Comparing	6 Speaking/Signalling	6 Feeding/Offbearing
	7 Serving	7 Handling
	8 Taking Instructions/Helping	

The worker functions code (267) may relate to any career group. These three middle digits, which can be part of the code for a real estate appraiser, indicate that the worker is *analyzing* in relation to data (2), *speaking/signalling* in relation to people (6), and *handling* in relation to things (7). The appraiser is near the top of the list requiring involvement with data but lower on the work performance lists involving people and things. The worker functions become progressively complex as the numbers in each group decrease.

The last three digits of the code number (010) indicate a specific career within a career group. For instance, many careers may have the same first six digits, but the last three digits differentiate one particular career from all others. If there is more than one career with the same first six digits, the last three digits are usually listed in alphabetical order of titles and by adding four to each new title (010, 014, 018, 022, 026, 030, and the like).

Compare the career code of a real estate appraiser to that of a credit analyst:

191.267-010   Real estate appraiser
191.267-014   Credit analyst

Tips for Self-Assessment

- What type of career do I want for myself; one that deals most with ideas, people, or things?
- Why do I want this type of career over the other two types?
- What qualities about me make this type of career suitable?

IDEAS, PEOPLE, AND THINGS CLASSIFICATION

Careers can be classified other ways. You may find it beneficial to divide careers into those which focus primarily on *ideas* (data), on *people,* or on *things.* The automobile upholsterer, the pharmaceutical-compounding supervisor, or the perforator typist, for example, work primarily with things or materials. Careers such as foreign-student advisor, dean of students, or criminal lawyer involve dealing with people. Archivists, curators, and tele-

Some careers involve working mainly with *data.*

vision directors are particularly interested in specific ideas. Mathematicians, writers, and musicians are careers which deal with more abstract ideas. Based on what you already know about careers, what you know of other workers, and your own work experience, you can name other careers related to each of the three categories.

By now, you probably have realized that most careers are not solely related to ideas, or to people, or to things. Rather, careers may be related to both people and things, or ideas and things, or people and ideas, or a combination of things, ideas, and people. The following list illustrates these four career relationships.

1. *People and Ideas*—budget officer, credit counselor, accounts receivable supervisor, contract administrator, senior reservations agent

© Linda Ammons

Some positions involve working primarily with *people*.

2. *Things and Ideas*—advertising statistical clerk, telegraph office telephone clerk, court clerk, media clerk, marine architect
3. *Things and People*—securities vault supervisor, communication center coordinator, general ledger bookkeeper, social secretary
4. *Ideas, People, and Things*—audit clerk supervisor, physical therapist, dietetic technician, medical technologist (teaching supervisor), podiatrist, medical physicist

You should also understand that many careers have either *direct* or *indirect contact* with people or things. Physical therapists have direct contact with their patients; whereas, newspaper editors have indirect contact with readers through their newspaper articles. Furriers and orthopedic shoe designers have direct contact with things, but bookkeepers have indirect contact with things through numerical figures.

As you consider your values, interests, lifestyle, strengths and weaknesses, you can decide whether you want to work with things, ideas, or people; however, remember the three categories overlap. Most careers involve dealing with people in one way or another. Many careers require you to use tools, equipment, or instruments. Try not to limit your career to only one category. Though you may prefer working with ideas, it is likely

Strix Pix

In other careers, you work with *things,* principally.

that you can identify career categories involving things and people which will also interest you.

CLASSIFYING CAREERS BY INDUSTRIES

Tips for Self-Assessment

- In what type of industries would I like to work?
- How do I see myself in those industries?
- How willing am I to switch from one industry to another?

The industrial classification of careers is mostly for governmental use; however, this classification can be beneficial in considering career options. As was suggested earlier, you generally develop specific career goals after exploring general areas of work. In some cases, a person might choose a career after first examining an industry.

Elizabeth, for instance, felt her career opportunities restricted because only two industries (agriculture and education) existed in her community. She decided to seek employment in a high-technology industry, but had little, if any, knowledge of the available entry level careers.

The following system is adapted from the 1972 *Standard Industrial Classification Manual,*[2] a method wherein careers are classified by industry. Industries are grouped according to the activities in which their workers are engaged.

Goods
Producing
Industries
{
1. Agriculture, forestry, and fisheries
2. Mining
3. Construction
4. Manufacturing
5. Transportation, communications, electric, gas, and sanitary services

Service
Producing
Industries
{
6. Wholesale trade
7. Retail trade
8. Finance, insurance, and real estate
9. Services
10. Public administration
11. Nonclassifiable establishments

Assume you are interested in the field of engineering. You would find this career in several industries described in the preceding list. You would then decide which industry you find most appealing. You could select transportation, finance, or perhaps services. Your final tasks would be to determine which industry is hiring managers and explore your chances of moving from one industry to another.

CLASSIFYING CAREERS BY DIVISION

The 1980 *Standard Occupational Classification Manual,* developed by the U.S. Department of Commerce, arranges careers into twenty-two divisions.[3] These divisions are further broken down into *major groups, minor groups,* and *unit groups.* To illustrate this arrangement, first consider several divisions of career groups.

Executive, administrative, and managerial
Engineers, surveyors, and architects
Natural scientists and mathematicians
Social scientists, social workers, religious workers, and lawyers
Teachers, librarians, and counselors
Health diagnosing and treating practitioners
Nurses, pharmacists, dietitians, therapists, and physicians' assistants
Writers, artists, entertainers, and athletes
Health technologists and technicians
Technologists and technicians, except health
Marketing and sales
Clerical

[2] U.S. Executive Office of the President, Office of Management and Budget, *Standard Industrial Classification Manual* (Washington, DC: Government Printing Office, 1972).

[3] U.S. Department of Commerce, *Standard Occupational Classification Manual* (Washington, DC: Government Printing Office, 1980).

Each division is broken down into *major groups*. For instance, if your career goal is in the natural scientists and mathematicians division, then you may want to explore careers within one of its major groups.

Division

Natural Scientists and Mathematicians

Major Group

Computer, mathematical, and operations research

Next, you might explore more specific careers from a *minor group*. An illustration of the minor group, under computer, mathematical, and operations research, is as follows:

Minor Group

Computer scientists
Operations and systems research analysts
Mathematical scientists
Physical scientists
Life scientists

Finally, you may focus your attention on a specific career group within the *minor group* called a *unit group*. This unit group lists specific careers, for example:

Minor Group

Computer scientists

Unit Group

Computer systems analyst
Systems analyst, electronic data processing, computer analyst
Computer-systems planning
Computer-systems analyst
Systems analyst, computer systems
Systems analyst, data processing

CAREER FAMILY CLASSIFICATIONS

Tips for Self-Assessment

- **What similarities might be used to group careers into *families*?**
- **How do I see myself in at least one career family?**

As mentioned earlier, many careers are closely related. Classifying careers by *career families*, sometimes referred to as *career clusters*, often helps you understand career relationships. Careers are often arranged in families on the basis of certain similarities, training requirements, and entry steps and levels.

OFFICE OF EDUCATION CLASSIFICATION

The U.S. Office of Education has developed a fifteen-career family classification system for educational programs. Each career family is arranged to include career advancement.[4]

Agribusiness and natural resources	Hospitality and recreation
Business and office	Manufacturing
Communications and media	Marketing and distribution
Construction	Marine science
Consumer and homemaking	Personal service
Environmental	Public service
Fine arts and humanities	Transportation
Health	

EIGHTEEN-FAMILY CLASSIFICATION

Thomas Harrington and Arthur O'Shea[5] have classified the career marketplace into eighteen families. Careers in each family contain the same combination of career interests. Medical-dental careers are grouped together since they require scientific and social service activities and interests. The following illustrates Harrington and O'Shea's eighteen career families:[6]

Skilled crafts	Management
Technical	Clerical work
Legal work	Medical-dental
Manual work	Personal service
Math–science	Sales work
Data analysis	Entertainment
Art work	Customer services
Literary work	Social services
Music work	Education work

If your goal is to attain a career in management, the Harrington and O'Shea career classification includes the following careers:[7]

Management

Contractor	Funeral director
Hotel/motel manager	Chief dietician
Restaurant manager	Hospital administrator
Sales manager	Radio-TV director
Store manager	Industrial engineer

[4]Neil A. Baker, Jr., *An Analysis of Fifteen Occupational Clusters Identified by the U.S. Department of Education* (Sherman/Denison, TX: Grayson City College, 1972).

[5]Thomas Harrington and Arthur O'Shea, *Career Decision-Making System* (Circle Pine, MN: American Guidance Service, 1982).

[6]Ibid., 2–3.

[7]Ibid.

CAREER FAMILIES FROM THE OCCUPATIONAL OUTLOOK HANDBOOK

The 1982–83 edition of the *Occupational Outlook Handbook* (OOH), prepared by the Bureau of Labor Statistics, U.S. Department of Labor, presents twenty career families.[8] Having identified your career interests, you might explore some of these families of related careers.

OOH Career Families

Administrative and managerial careers
Engineers, surveyors, and architects
Natural scientists and mathematicians
Social scientists, social workers, religious workers, and lawyers
Teachers, librarians, and counselors
Health diagnosing and treating practitioners
Registered nurses, pharmacists, dieticians, therapists, and
   physician's assistants
Health technologists and technicians
Writers, artists, and entertainers
Technologists and technicians, except health, marketing, and sales careers
Administrative support occupations, including clerical
Service careers
Agricultural and forestry careers
Mechanics and repairers
Construction and extractive careers
Production careers
Transportation and material moving careers
Helpers, handlers, equipment cleaners, and laborers
Military careers

Should you find that you like caring for other people, you might begin by exploring careers in three health career families. Or, if you like driving motor vehicles, you may start examining careers in the transportation and material moving careers family.

CLASSIFICATION BY CAREER ENVIRONMENT

Another career family classification system is based on John Holland's six orientation-work environments (discussed in Chapter 2). These career environments describe six areas.[9]

R   *Realistic career environment*—service, technical, and skills trade careers
I   *Investigative career environment*—scientific and technical careers
A   *Artistic career environment*—literary, artistic, and musical careers
S   *Social career environment*—social welfare and educational careers
E   *Enterprising career environment*—sales and managerial careers
C   *Conventional career environment*—clerical and office careers

[8]U.S. Department of Labor, *Occupational Outlook Handbook* (Washington, DC: U.S. Government Printing Office, 1982–83).

[9]John L. Holland, *Making Vocational Choices: A Theory of Careers*, 2nd ed. (Englewood Cliffs, NJ: Prentice-Hall, 1985).

John Holland describes this classification system in the *Self-Directed Search* as a self-administered and interpreted inventory for educational and career planning.[10] Your findings from the *Self-Directed Search* present your three most dominant personal orientations within Holland's classification system. For example, the dominant three-letter code, ESC, indicates Enterprising, Social, and Conventional orientations, with Enterprising being most dominant. The career clusters for each three-letter code appear in Holland's *Occupations Finder*. The following are examples of career clusters under each three-letter code.[11]

	ED
CODE: RIA	
Landscape Architect (001.061-018)	5
Architectural Drafter (001.261-010)	4
Dental Technician (712.381-018)	4
CODE: AIR	ED
Architect (001.061-010)	6
Photographer (143.457.010)	4
Photolithographer (972.382-014)	4
Sign Writer (970.281-022)	4
Photograph Retoucher (970.281-018)	3
CODE: SAC	ED
Cosmetologist (332.271-010)	4
Electrologist (339.371-010)	4
Embalmer (338.371-014)	4
Hair Stylist (332.271-018)	4
Physical Therapy Aide (335.354-010)	3

This preceding system includes classification codes from the fourth edition of the *Dictionary of Occupational Titles* and the corresponding level of education required for each career. Procedures for using this system are provided in the *Self-Directed Search*.

The single digits in the preceding column to the right (ED) indicate the general level of education a career demands. Levels 5 and 6 mean college training is necessary. Levels 3 and 4 mean high school and some college, technical, or business training is needed. Generally, these levels are only estimates, not definite requirements.

GOE CAREER CLASSIFICATIONS

In 1979 the United States Employment Service designed the original *Guide for Occupational Exploration (GOE)* to assist career seekers in exploring various fields. The 1984 edition of the *GOE*, a revised guide, edited by

---

[10]John L. Holland, *Self-Directed Search: A Guide to Educational and Vocational Planning* (Palo Alto, CA: Consulting Psychologist Press, 1984).

[11]John L. Holland, *The Occupations Finder* (Palo Alto, CA: Consulting Psychologist Press, 1984), 2, 3, 5, 7.

Thomas F. Harrington and Arthur J. O'Shea,[12] presents *career clues,* such as work values, hobbies and leisure activities, home-related activities, and school subjects. This revised guide relates each clue to the pertinent work groups in the text. Additionally, the *GOE* relates work experience and military career specialties to career selection. The second edition includes aids which assist the reader in identifying interests, values, and experiences, as well as associate them with appropriate career fields.

The 1979 edition of the *GOE* classifies all careers listed in the *Dictionary of Occupational Titles* (excluding military careers) into 12 interest areas, 66 work groups, and various subgroups within each work group. The revised guide retains this classification system of interest areas, work groups, and subgroups but provides more information than does the 1979 *GOE.* The 1984 *GOE* identifies twelve interest areas by a two-digit code along with a title, for example:

01	Artistic	05	Mechanical	09	Accommodating
02	Scientific	06	Industrial	10	Humanitarian
03	Plants and Animals	07	Business Details	11	Leading Influences
04	Protective	08	Selling	12	Physical Performing

These twelve interest areas are further divided into sixty-six work groups. Each work group has a four-digit code and title.

02.01	Physical Sciences
04.01	Safety and Law Enforcement
05.01	Engineering
06.01	Production Technology

The number of work groups in each interest area can vary from two to twelve groups. The groups requiring more education, training, and experience appear first, and other groups, with requirements under each interest area, follow in descending order.

Since some of the work groups include many occupations, these groups are divided into subgroups. A six-digit code and a title indicate each subgroup.

Interest area	—	05	Mechanical
Work Group	—	05.01	Engineering
Subgroups	—	05.01.01	Research
		05.01.02	Environmental Protection
		05.01.03	Systems Design
		05.01.04	Testing and Quality Control
		05.01.05	Sales Engineering
		05.01.06	Work Planning and Utilization
		05.01.07	Design
		05.01.08	General Engineering

---

[12]Thomas F. Harrington and Arthur J. O'Shea, eds., *Guide for Occupational Exploration,* 2nd ed. (Circle Pines, MN: American Guidance Service, 1984).

The subgrouping differs from one work group to another. The subgroups in 05.01, for example, pertain to engineering, while the 11.11 subgroups pertain to business management.

Because of the large number of careers within some of the subgroups, these careers are further grouped by industry. Examples of such industry subgroups are agricultural equipment, aircraft-aerospace, manufacturing and air transportation industries. Under industry subgroups, careers appear in alphabetical order. If a career might appear under more than one industry, it is listed according to the first alphabetical listing. For instance, a career having the designations iron and steel and non-ferrous metal alloys would be listed under *iron and steel.*

Each career has a letter code which represents the physical strength required while performing in that career, as shown in Table 4-1..

The level of training in mathematics and language also is provided in the description for each career. A brief explanation of the training levels appears in Table 4-2.

You should recognize that changing conditions in today's economy or a change within yourself may cause you to alter your career goals either before starting a career or after several years of working. Suppose you are interested in health service careers. Perhaps your goal is to be a gynecologist (a physician specializing in diagnosing and treating female diseases and disorders), but something happens which prevents you from completing your training. As a result, you explore the other careers in the health service family until you identify one which seems appropriate for your level of training. Or, say you have been working for the past four years at IBM in accounting, but now you feel dissatisfied. If you understand career clusters, you will frequently find it possible to transfer to another career in the same family. There you can apply your skills and benefit from your previous career experiences and education.

Career and industrial classification systems help you learn about the world of work. Frequently you choose a career goal as you explore broad career fields.

Obviously, it is unrealistic for you to be knowledgable of all careers. To minimize your efforts in becoming acquainted with the structure of the

TABLE 4-1   **Strength factor codes**

Code	Description	Maximum Weight Lifted	Weight Frequently Lifted and Carried
S	Sedentary	10 pounds	—
L	Light	20 pounds	Up to 10 pounds
M	Medium	50 pounds	Up to 25 pounds
H	Heavy	100 pounds	Up to 50 pounds
V	Very heavy	Over 100 pounds	Over 50 pounds

SOURCE: Harrington and O'Shea, *Guide for Occupational Exploration,* 77.

TABLE 4-2   Specific career preparation training codes

Level	Length of Training
9	Over 10 years
8	4 to 10 years
7	2 to 4 years
6	1 to 2 years
5	6 months to 1 year
4	3 to 6 months
3	1 to 3 months
2	Less than 1 month
1	Short demonstration

SOURCE: Harrington and O'Shea, *Guide for Occupational Exploration*, 79.

world of work, consider various career classification systems. None of these classification systems is necessarily better than another. Therefore, explore several of them and then use the one that seems most appropriate.

Since you may make career decisions more than once in your lifetime, you may also frequently use career classifications. As you move up the career ladder or perhaps laterally to another field, you can base your decisions on information rather than rely on chance.

POINTS TO REVIEW

1. Career classification systems help you understand the relationships between and among various careers.
2. Being aware of the organizational classifications may help you explore and choose a specific career.
3. Many systems classify careers into groups.
4. The U.S. Department of Labor classifies careers into career categories, divisions, and groups.
5. These career categories are professional, technical, and managerial careers; clerical and sales careers; service careers; agricultural careers; fishery careers; bench work careers; structural work careers; and miscellaneous careers.
6. The *Standard Industrial Classification Manual* classifies industries into eleven separate groups.
7. The 1983 edition of the *Standard Occupational Classification Manual* arranges careers into twenty-two divisions of career groups. The divisions are further broken down into major, minor, and unit groups.
8. Careers can also be classified into ideas, people, and things; however, most careers are not *solely* associated with ideas, or people, or things.

9. Many careers deal with both people and things, or with ideas and things, or with people and ideas, or a combination of all three.

10. Careers can be classified into families according to similarities, training requirements, and entry steps and levels.

11. One career family classification system, based on Holland's career environments, groups careers into the following career families: realistic, investigative, artistic, social, enterprising, and conventional.

Experiential Exercises

1. Describe each *career category* by matching the *types of work* which a person might perform in that field.

	Types of Work		Career Categories
a.	protection for people and property	_____	professional, technical and managerial
b.	transcribing and·systematizing	_____	clerical and sales
c.	mixing, chemically treating, and refining	_____	agriculture, fishery, forestry
d.	installation, repair, and reassembly	_____	service
e.	transporting people, packaging materials	_____	processing
f.	paving, erecting, fabricating	_____	machine trade
g.	growing, logging, catching	_____	bench work
h.	teaching, piloting aircraft	_____	structural work
i.	inspecting, repairing small items	_____	miscellaneous

2. Use a check mark (√) to indicate which industries produce goods and which produce services.

Industries	Produces Goods	Produces Services
a. Agriculture, forestry, and fishery		
b. Mining		
c. Construction		
d. Manufacturing		
e. Transportation, communication		
f. Wholesale trade		
g. Retail trade		
h. Finance, insurance, and real estate		
i. Public administration		

To enlarge your career alternatives list, engage others in the following brainstorming activities.

3. List three careers that deal primarily with the following categories:

a. Ideas   _____   _____   _____

b. People   _____   _____   _____

c. Things   _____   _____   _____

d. Ideas and People   _____   _____   _____

e. Things and Ideas   _____   _____   _____

f. Things and People   _____   _____   _____

g. Ideas, People,
   and Things   _____   _____   _____

4. With which of following would you prefer to work? To indicate your choice, place a *1* next to your first choice, a *2* next to your second choice, and a *3* next to your final choice.

   Ideas (Data)   _____

   People   _____

   Things   _____

5. Various career fields follow:

Skilled crafts	Art	Personal service
Technical work	Literary work	Sales
Legal work	Music	Entertainment
Manual labor	Management	Customer services
Math-science	Clerical work	Social services
Data analysis	Medical-dental	Education

   List as many as three fields that interest you, with *1.* indicating your first choice, *2.* your second choice, and *3.* your third choice.

   1. _____

   2. _____

   3. _____

6. What type of work environment would you most prefer? Indicate your first, second, and third choices by placing the numbers *1, 2,* and *3* in the blank spaces next to your chosen work environments.

   Realistic _____   Social _____

   Investigative _____   Enterprising _____

   Artistic _____   Conventional _____

5

Checking out preferred career choices can lead to positive work adjustment and career satisfaction.

Exploring Possible Careers

Examining the classification systems of the career marketplace is an important step in developing your personal vocational interests; however, sound, realistic decisions require seeking out additional information on the choices you have made or stand ready to make. At this point your choices should only be tentative. Still, considering only your personal preference for certain career areas may limit you and lead you to overlook other important factors, such as (a) the nature of the work; (b) mental, physical aptitudes, personality; (c) education, training, and other entry requirements of the job; (d) restrictions affecting eligibility for that career; (e) working conditions; (f) supply and demand of workers in that field; and (g) the income, chance for promotion, and security a certain job offers.

Because answers to questions like these often are not considered in career selections, individuals sometimes experience a great deal of mental and physical stress at work, a frustrating inability to cope with the demands placed upon them, a pervasive dissatisfaction with their work and themselves, and a general restlessness in life, perpetually shifting from one job to the next. The aim of this chapter is to discuss the factors you need to consider to make good choices that will lead to positive career adjustment and satisfaction in life. Additionally, the chapter includes a list and profile of various sources of information on careers.

WORK ADJUSTMENT AND CAREER SATISFACTION

Tips for Self-Assessment

- As I think about a specific career, what factors must that job include to meet my needs?
- How will I meet the needs of my work environment?

Your work adjustment and satisfaction with your chosen career are all-important considerations in lifelong career planning. Your suitability to the work environment and of the work environment's basic *rightness* for you can determine how well you adjust to your career. You must bring certain skills to the work environment—say, hypothetically, scientific skills to work

© Linda Ammons

Good career choices can lead to satisfaction in your work and in your life.

at the Unison Pharmaceutical Laboratory. The laboratory work environment provides you with certain rewards (salary, prestige, social relations). Your skills permit you in turn to meet the requirements of that work environment. The rewards gained from the laboratory environment fulfill your personal requirements. With the laboratory's and your own requirements mutually fulfilled, you and that workplace can be described as a suitable match.

When you entered Unison Pharmaceutical Laboratory for the first time, you focused your goals on meeting its job requirements. Finding a suitable relationship between yourself and that organization, you strove to maintain it. Should that relationship not have been suitable, you would have attempted to improve it; that effort proving unsuccessful, you might well have moved out of pharmaceuticals to another work environment.

Your work satisfaction is a basic indicator of the degree of success you have obtained in maintaining a positive relationship between yourself and your work environment. Sources of appraisal of that relationship are either external or internal. First, factors outside, or other than, you (your supervisors and your co-workers) judge how well you meet the requirements of the work environment. In the second case, you appraise how perfectly the work environment meets your requirements.

You should carefully consider a variety of factors when choosing a career. Your career adjustment and satisfaction may vary from one work environment to the next, but you can maximize the relationship between you as a worker and your work setting by first carefully studying the ins-and-outs of your career choice(s).

FACTORS TO CONSIDER WHEN STUDYING CAREERS

Assume that you have explored a wide variety of available careers and have narrowed your options to three or four vocations. You now need to attain extensive, accurate information about these careers. In studying them, keep in mind at least nine essential matters of interest:

Nature of the career	Opportunities for advancement
Personal quality requirements	Working conditions
Educational and training requirements	Competition
Entry requirements	Earnings
Opportunities for transfer	

NATURE OF THE CAREER

Obviously, one of the first things you want to learn about is the nature of the work you will be expected to perform within your preferred career. What activities, functions, and responsibilities does this career entail? You will need to decide whether or not the work performed actually appeals to

Tips for Self-Assessment

- What type of work do I want as my career?
- Why does the nature of this work appeal to me?
- Does this career appeal because it offers present, short-range, or long-range rewards?

you. Also, you need to discover what specific tasks the workers perform, what equipment or tools they use, and how they perform the tasks. In sources providing career definitions (e.g. *Dictionary of Occupational Titles*), additional information describes what gets done, how, and why. For example:

> CATALOGER (library) catalog librarian; descriptive cataloger. Compiles information on library materials, such as books, and periodicals, and prepares catalog cards to identify materials and to integrate information into library catalog. Verifies author, title, and classification number . . . .[1]

Descriptions also provide other types of information, such as functions performed by the worker. You might focus on the relationship between the worker's functions and ideas (data), people, and things, to identify levels at which the career would require you to function. Note the following job description:

> PHYSICIST, THEORETICAL. Interprets results of experiments in physics, formulates theories consistent with data obtained, and predicts results of experiments designed to detect and . . . .[2]

You might also consider what interests underlie a career. Observe the interests in this example:

> EDITORIAL WRITER. Writes comments on topics of current interest to stimulate or mold public opinion in accordance with viewpoints and policies of publication . . . .[3]

Information dealing with the what, why, and how of your selected career field will provide a broader picture of the nature of work within these fields. Yet, you should remember that your own work activities may depend upon your specific work setting.

PERSONAL QUALITY REQUIREMENTS

Your unique characteristics can be essential to career performance. How well your personal qualities match the requirements of careers which interest you may determine your personal satisfaction, as well as your chance to succeed. Some careers require workers to be energetic; others

---

[1] U.S. Department of Labor, *Dictionary of Occupational Titles*, 4th ed. (Washington, DC: U.S. Government Printing Office, 1977), 73.

[2] Ibid., 40.

[3] Ibid., 77–78.

Tips for Self-Assessment

- How would I describe my personal qualities?
- What aspects of my personality will satisfy the requirements of the careers which interest me?
- To what extent can I adjust or improve my personality in areas where I am weak?
- How realistic am I as I evaluate both my personality and career requirements?

require individuals to be precise. Usually a combination of characteristics may be essential for achieving and maintaining work goals.

Examine your preferred careers to see which personal qualities they require and if these qualities are like your own. Some sales careers require you to be persuasive, sociable, or persistent; whereas, accounting positions demand that you pay careful attention to details. Customer service usually requires courtesy and tact in dealing with people, while accommodations work requires a pleasant personality, poise, good manners, good grooming, or conversational ability. A police officer must be motivated, self-disciplined, cool-headed, and honest. After considering these few careers and their expectations, explore the personality requirements of other careers as they relate to your own personality.

Sort out potential careers which have personality expectations similar to your own or careers which foster a lifestyle you would like. Your personality may determine whether you attain, hold, or advance your career. Suitability between your personality and career interests will contribute to work satisfaction. Note, though, in order to explore personality requirements of careers, you should understand yourself.

EDUCATIONAL AND TRAINING REQUIREMENTS

Tips for Self-Assessment

- How much education and/or training will I need to attain my preferred career?
- How committed am I to investing my time to education and/or training?
- Without this commitment, what options are available to me?

When exploring possible vocations, seek answers to such questions as: "What kind of education is expected for this position?" "Do I need professional, technical, or general education?" Educational requirements for entry-level positions range from high school, technical training, and college (with a two-year associate degree or bachelor's degree) to graduate study (with a master's degree or doctorate). You can prepare for a career through college study; postsecondary vocational-technical school; home study; government training; experience or training obtained in the U.S. Armed Forces; apprenticeship and other formal training offered by employers; and high school courses. Keep in mind that your education and training, in many cases, will determine the level at which you enter a career and the time you must take to advance up the career ladder. Consider the educational and training requirements for an FBI special agent.

> The minimal education standards that are required for acceptance as an FBI agent are either a degree from a state-accredited law school or a college degree with an accounting major. People with other special skills, such as scientific knowledge, foreign language proficiency, or years of executive experience, are occasionally accepted as special agents as the need arises for them.
>
> All applicants must be at least twenty-three years old, less than thirty-five, United States citizens, and physically capable of fulfilling stringent requirements set by the Bureau. They are tested intensively both orally and in writing, and their background is closely investigated by agents of the Bureau. All appointments are made on a one-year probationary basis, becoming confirmed after that time if performance is satisfactory.
>
> New agents are given fifteen weeks of intensive instruction in the techniques essential to their jobs as well as Federal criminal law and procedures at the FBI academy.[4]

You may need to focus on a necessary apprenticeship or internship to enter a specific career field. Public school teachers, school administrators, medical doctors, and clinical psychologists are required to serve an internship. Some businesses and local union management committees provide opportunities for apprenticeships in underwriting, hotel management, brick laying, plumbing, and pipefitting.

Keep in mind other questions as you explore selected career fields. Are there a limited number of persons admitted to special training? What is the length of time required for training in school and/or working in a particular career field? How much will the required training cost for a certain career? These questions regarding educational and training expectations can help you select appropriate career fields.

ENTRY REQUIREMENTS

Tips for Self-Assessment

- How willing am I to meet requirements beyond my education and training?
- How comfortable am I about taking an examination to enter a field?
- If I am uncomfortable, how can I change my feelings about examinations for career entry?
- What alternatives do I have?

[4]David M. Brownstone and Gene A. Hawes, *The Complete Career Guide* (New York: Simon and Schuster, 1978), 193.

Must you meet license or certification requirements before you can work in a chosen career? In many fields, education and training are not sufficient qualifications for practicing a career. For instance, many states in the United States require you obtain a license or certificate to qualify and practice a career. Some states even require potential professionals, provided they have completed their education or required internship, to take an examination in their respective career before practicing in that field. Consider state requirements in the following example.

Real Estate Agents or Brokers

All states require prospective agents to be a high school graduate, be at least 18 years old, and pass a written test. The examination—more comprehensive for brokers than for agents—includes questions on basic real estate transactions and on laws affecting the sale of property. Most states require candidates for the general sales license to complete at least 30 hours of classroom instruction and those seeking the broker's license to complete 90 hours of formal training in addition to a specified amount of experience in selling real estate (generally 1 to 3 years). Some states waive the experience requirements for the broker's license for applicants who have a bachelor's degree in real estate. State licenses generally must be renewed every year or two, however, some require continuing education for license renewal.[5]

Accountants who desire to be a CPA (Certified Public Accountant) can obtain a certificate by passing rigorous examinations and meeting the educational and experience requirements prescribed by law in each state. Most communities require plumbers to be licensed. These workers may obtain their license by passing a special examination to demonstrate knowledge of the trade and the local plumbing codes. Note that many workers do not have to obtain a state license or certificate. Such careers would include fashion modeling, retail sales, and photography.

Applications for license examinations are often available through state department agencies and professional organizations. Applicants usually must pay certain fees to take these tests.

In many fields, union or professional organization membership is required. Other vocations may encourage such membership but not require it. Still other career fields are not affiliated with either a union or a professional group.

OPPORTUNITIES FOR TRANSFER

Tips for Self-Assessment

- My career may be satisfying now, but what might occur to make me want to change positions?
- To what degree will my career field allow me to enter another in the future?

[5]Department of Labor, Bureau of Labor Statistics, *Occupational Outlook Handbook, 1982–1983* (Washington, DC: U.S. Government Printing Office, 1982), 248.

Since both you and the marketplace change over time, consider your opportunities to switch to other careers, as you explore those fields most interesting to you. Right now you may be thinking, "as hard as work is to find, I wouldn't dare consider moving to another position, once I get into the field I like." While this may sound realistic because of present circumstances, changes within yourself and in the marketplace may alter that decision. Therefore, explore each career with a view toward the future and determine whether a specific career will allow you to move into related careers.

For example, broadcasting engineers work with their hands and are knowledgable about electronics. With little, if any, additional training, engineers can switch to several types of electronic repair or construction businesses. Possibly engineers can attain teaching positions in technical schools.

Copywriters have gone into other related careers. Some have written books, and others have switched to public relations positions. It is not uncommon for copywriters to be offered administrative positions after having worked for certain accounts. Some copywriters may do consulting; others have teaching positions.

These examples show how one career may lead to another position. The advantage of recognizing possibilities for career change is that you are planning not only for the present, but also for the future.

OPPORTUNITIES FOR ADVANCEMENT

Most workers do not begin their career at top levels; they start in low- to middle-level positions. You should examine various careers thinking that in the future you may want to move up the career ladder. A medical records administrator position can lead to a higher management position, such as hospital administrator. Clear paths for advancement exist in the field of occupational therapy. For instance, an occupational therapist might move to a supervisory or administrative position. A salesperson working in a company may advance to manager and later to general manager. An occupational safety and health worker who works in a factory can move into the supervisory position of plant safety and health manager. In an insurance company, one might advance from managing a small office, to managing a regional office, or to heading administration in the company headquarters. Advancement in many careers is contingent upon developing your own practice or business, while advancement in other fields requires developing professional skills, assuming greater responsibilities, or directing a particular division (department).

In short, identify and evaluate each career path which offers possibilities for upward career movement. Advancement paths in some fields are more well-defined than in others. Ask yourself where you would like to be in your career, say, four or five years from now, and ask yourself if your career will offer you a path to achieve your goal.

WORKING CONDITIONS

Tips for Self-Assessment

- What kind of working conditions do I prefer?
- How realistic are my preferred working conditions compared to actual working conditions in my career field?
- How might I modify my working conditions, if they were the only aspect of a position I found dissatisfying?
- How can I prepare myself to deal effectively with a variety of working conditions?

When you explore careers, consider conditions under which you may have to work. Various working conditions may be attractive, while others will be less attractive. Most jobs include both conditions. By carefully exploring careers, you will be able to maximize your options for those with the more appealing conditions.

As you explore, be concerned about the length of the workday, whether the hours are regular or irregular, if there is any or much overtime, and the periods when the work is particularly heavy. Many police officers, fast-food workers, industrial security guards, nurses, grocery store clerks, and assembly-line workers are required to work evenings or nights as part of a rotating schedule. Some workers, like taxi and bus drivers, must work split-shifts—morning and then early afternoons. Consider the working hours of each career to find the one which best matches your interest.

Many careers require outdoor work; others require indoor work. Sanitation workers, mail carriers, and highway construction workers spend much of their time outside. These workers face different weather conditions, but may prefer outdoor over indoor work. (Note that the higher your educational level, the more likely you will prefer working indoors.)

Another factor to consider is work environment. Do you prefer traveling in a jet, ship, or car? Do you prefer working around a large number of people or a few others? Some people do not mind working in dusty, oily, or odorous settings. By being aware of work settings, you can select environments which appeal to you.

How safe are the careers which interest you? Will you have to be concerned about cuts, burns, bruises, or even falls (in repair shops, factories, restaurant kitchens, or construction sites)? To make sure you are protected, your employer may expect you to wear protective clothing and equipment.

Many careers require you stand, while others require you sit for long periods. Some careers demand that you work crouching in awkward positions or engage in strenuous physical activities.

Other conditions to consider are working under tension; working against time; experiencing an uneven pace of work activities; changing work procedures; working alone or with several others; working independently or under close supervision; having responsibility for supervising others;

Many people prefer a clean, pleasant work environment.

Some people don't mind getting dirty to make some money.

and working with your hands, mind, or both. Identifying these, among other concerns, will enable you to evaluate each career thoroughly.

COMPETITION

Tips for Self-Assessment

- In what ways does competition influence my work?
- How willing am I to compete in an over-crowded field, for example law or medicine?

You must consider still other factors when exploring careers. What demand exists for new workers—men and women—in this field, and how much competition will you have? What is the outlook of this career for the future? What developing technologies and other factors will influence the growth (or decline) of this career? Information regarding career prospects can be valuable. In some fields demand for workers can be so great, and the supply so limited, that even the marginal worker has a fair chance of obtaining work. An individual looking for even temporary work may have few problems obtaining a position.

Our nation's economy, technological development, legislative decisions, and change within the population all influence the demand for workers. Job prospects in a particular field may depend upon ethnicity, age, sex, education, training, or other expectations. The number of workers presently employed in a given career field generally suggests future job prospects in that field. The number of jobs in public school teaching is greater than in dentistry, for example. Often a greater demand exists for specialized careers than for others within the same field.

The Department of Labor[6] reports that careers in the civilian labor force are projected to increase to 108.6 million by 1985, and to 113.8 million by 1990 (see Table 5–1). The number of women joining the labor force has been rapidly increasing, and this rise is predicted to continue, although at a lower rate, through 1990. The number of women in the marketplace (37.0 million in 1975) is projected to increase by 11.6 million by 1990, an increase of 1.8 percent per year. The number of men in the marketplace (55.6 million in 1975) is expected to grow by 9.6 million between 1975 and 1990, an increase of 1.1 percent a year; however, men are expected to comprise more than half (57 percent) of the civilian labor force in 1990. The number of youths participating in the labor force is actually expected to decline by 1985 and decline further by 1990. These shrinking figures will first apply to teenagers and later to youths 20 to 24 years of age. During the early 1980s, employment figures should change very little, with decreases in the number of older men in the marketplace offset by increases in the number of older women. In the late 1980s the number of persons age 55 and over in the

[6]U.S. Department of Labor, Bureau of Labor and Statistics, *New Labor Force Projections to 1990, Special Labor Force Report 1977* (Washington, DC: U.S. Government Printing Office, 1977).

TABLE 5-1 **Projections of the size and participation rate of the labor force**

	Civilian Labor Force Annual Average Size		Civilian Labor Force Participation Rates (Percent of Population in Labor Force)	
	1985	1990	1985	1990
Total Civilian Labor Force	108,602	113,839	63.2	63.6
Men				
16–19 years	4,181	3,976	60.9	61.3
20–24	7,795	6,671	83.0	82.1
25–34	18,021	18,545	94.9	94.7
35–44	14,192	16,572	95.1	94.8
45–54	9,709	10,901	90.6	90.2
55–64	7,162	6,704	71.6	69.9
65 and over	1,843	1,852	18.0	16.8
Women				
16–19 years	3,762	3,549	53.6	55.2
20–24	7,329	6,656	72.5	75.2
25–34	12,210	13,077	61.2	63.5
35–44	9,723	11,678	61.1	63.0
45–54	6,761	7,795	59.1	60.3
55–64	4,740	4,514	42.2	42.3
65 and over	1,174	1,250	7.8	7.6

SOURCE: Adapted from the Department of Labor, Bureau of Labor Statistics, *Labor Force Projections to 1990, Special Labor Force Report 1977.*

marketplace is projected to fall, and the 1990 level of 14.3 million should be only slightly higher than the 1975 average for this group. This decline is probably a short-term phenomenon, related to a decline in the population age range 54 to 64.

The career market is expected to grow 19 percent by 1995; however, the number of workers aged 25 to 44 (including most of the baby boomers) will rise to nearly 25 percent.[7] According to Raymond Ewing, issues management director for Allstate Insurance, the 2,000 largest U.S. corporations plan to hire approximately 10,000 persons in issues management. A sizeable number of women have already established a foothold within this field. (Women make up a quarter of the 400 members of the newly formed Issues Management Association.[8])

Century 21, a real estate company, has planned to increase its 60,000 employees by 20,000 in 1983 and another 80,000 by 1987.[9] While most of these added persons will work in real estate sales, others will deal with property management, develop syndications (combinations of persons or companies formed to carry out a business undertaking), and arrange mortgages.

[7]Patricia O'Toole, "Finding Work in Glutted Fields," *Money,* 12 (March, 1983): 67–68, 70, 72.
[8]Ibid., 67.
[9]Candace E. Trunzo, "Careers That Are Revving Up," *Money,* 12 (May, 1983): 92.

The U.S. Bureau of Labor and Statistics[10] projects that the figures representing hiring in sales will grow more rapidly than the average for all careers within the next ten years. By 1990, more than one million new sales careers will be available.

Career specialists or counselors often encourage individuals to consider high-tech (technological) careers—computers, biotechnology, genetic engineering, or robotics. Many people are rushing to enter these high-tech areas; however, present patterns indicate a renewing demand for personal services—high-touch professions. For example, Patricia O'Toole says:

> With the number of Americans over age 75 expected to rise nearly 75% by the year 2000, the high-touch career likely to expand fastest is gerontological nursing, where salaries start around $18,000. But the sleeper among service occupations may well be teaching, especially outside the public schools and the colleges. Millions of computer buyers will need instruction and so will millions of semiliterate workers. So many high school graduates these days are poor at English and math that well over 300 corporations run remedial classes. Large banks and insurance companies provide the most remedial education, and the person likely to do the hiring is the director of training and development.[11]

Candace E. Trunzo makes a similar remark regarding high-touch careers and the influence they will have on work.

> With the 65-and-over group expanding more rapidly than the population as a whole, the need will grow for business consultants who do retirement counseling and pension planning. More and more people will be required to provide health care for the aged. A Rand Corporation study projects a need for 8,000 to 9,000 geriatric doctors by 1990; only a few hundred doctors now practice this specialty. The need will be even greater for geriatric social workers who can attend to the nonmedical needs of the aged.[12]

One of the most unproductive strategies to consider is making your career choice based on the outlook for that career. A better strategy is to identify future changes and then determine where your abilities and interests will best match selected careers. Once you make your choice, remain flexible so that you can move into other careers at a later time. Fast changes in the current market suggest that there is little, if any, assurance you can stay in the same career throughout your lifetime. You might consider training as a generalist, who can adapt to a variety of career situations, instead of as a specialist, who may soon become obsolete.

Finally, when studying careers, be aware that national labor projections may cast a dim picture of job opportunities in your own community. That is, projected careers for the nation or a particular region, such as the Sunbelt, may not necessarily be the same for your community. Career projections for technical fields can also be misleading because they sometimes underestimate the required time for new technologies to spread

---

[10]U.S. Department of Labor, *Special Labor Force Report* 1977.

[11]O'Toole, "Finding Work," 68.

[12]Trunzo, "Careers Revving Up," 92.

within the marketplace. For instance, genetic engineering is creating considerably less work than was originally expected. Also, present conditions in the robotics field cast some doubt on the probability that this field will explode by 1990, as had earlier been expected.

EARNINGS

Tips for Self-Assessment

- As I enter a career, will my earnings support my lifestyle?
- What yearly salary do I want to earn?
- What yearly salary do I want to be earning ten years from now?
- How realistic are my career income expectations?
- If I cannot achieve my income expectations, what ideas might I then consider?
- In what way would income lead to my personal satisfaction?

While some persons are unconcerned with their income, many others give much attention to how much money they can earn in a given career. You might ask yourself questions such as: What salary can I expect to make as I begin my work? In what income range do the largest number of employees fall? What income can I expect to be making after one year (five years)? Will my income maintain my lifestyle? As I gain work experience, will my salary increase? Which areas in the United States (or which industries) offer the highest income for a particular type of work?

As you explore careers, consider both your salary (or wage) and your fringe benefits (a pension, paid holiday, or health insurance, which your employer covers). These fringe benefits frequently are a significant part of your overall earnings.

Employers often pay their workers salary wages. Many people who work irregular hours, weekends, holidays, night shifts, or overtime receive a pay differential—additional income for working outside the normal work schedule.

Pay levels vary within each career. Experienced workers almost always earn more than beginning workers. Also, income in a career field will differ by geographical location. For example, the average weekly income for beginning computer programmers varies from city to city, region to region. You should note that many locations offer high-income careers because those locations are more expensive to live in than others. Salaries also differ by career specialty or type of work performed. Surgeons, generally, earn more than other physicians.

While income is important to consider while selecting a career, you should not choose a career solely on the income it provides. Carefully considering earnings is but one step which can lead to career satisfaction.

SOURCES OF INFORMATION ABOUT CAREERS

Various sources describe careers. You can gather much information from such sources as books and pamphlets, places, and persons, and there find information about working conditions, job requirements, career outlook, physical demands of careers, earnings, and places of employment. The following examples list possible sources of career information. These materials may be obtained from a public or college library and career counselors.

Dictionary of Occupational Titles, 4th ed.
United States Department of Labor
Bureau of Labor Statistics
U.S. Government Printing Office
Washington, DC 20402

This text describes various career groups and contains related information for twenty thousand careers.

Occupational Outlook Handbook
U.S. Department of Labor
Superintendent of Documents
U.S. Government Printing Office
Washington, DC 20402

More than 800 careers in thirty families are listed, along with descriptions of work, training, education, and other requirements. The book also projects the outlook for employment demands.

Guide for Occupational Exploration
U.S. Department of Labor
Superintendent of Documents
U.S. Government Printing Office
Washington, DC 20402

This text is designed to help the reader realistically evaluate how her abilities may meet career requirements. This source provides information about interests, aptitudes, and skills requisite for career groups.

Guide for Occupational Exploration, 2nd ed.
American Guidance Service
Publishers' Building
Circle Pines, Minnesota 55018

This second edition (1984) is designed to help individuals arrive at an appropriate career decision, either with the assistance of a professional career specialist or through self-exploration. The guide presents information about work activities, physical demands, work environments, preparation required, and other characteristics of career groups. It encourages readers to compare these requirements with information they have about themselves.

Encyclopedia of Careers and Vocational Guidance, 3rd ed., Volumes I and II
Doubleday and Company
Garden City, NY 11530

Volume I provides information about several areas of work; Volume II contains information detailing specific careers.

Occupational View Deck
Chronical Guidance Publication
Moravia, New York 13118

This material explores various careers and their relationships to personal characteristics and preferences.

*Directory of Internships, Work Experience Programs and
    On-The-Job Training Opportunities*
Ready Reference Press
Thousand Oaks, CA 91360

The directory is a guide to thousands of new and continuing internship and employment opportunities supported by government agencies, business and industry, professional associations, foundations, and community organizations.

I Can Be Anything: Careers and Colleges for Young Women
College Entrance Examination Board
888 Seventh Avenue
New York, NY 10019

This guide provides information concerning various careers which women can enter. Each career description includes work activities, educational requirements, number of women in the field, salary range, projections for openings in the career, and names of people or organizations to contact for more information.

Many career market materials from the federal government (and other publishers) are useful. Yet, says W. Clyde Helms Jr., president of Occupational Forcasting Inc., a consulting firm in Arlington, Va.,

> the Department of Labor's *Dictionary of Occupational Titles* has become a dictionary of misinformation, and the Bureau of Labor Statistics offers less guidance than Magellan had when he sailed from Spain. Both sources are full of occupations that no longer exist, and both fail to mention many new fields, such as robotics and hazardous-waste management.[13]

To avoid using misleading career projections, you must thoroughly evaluate sources of information before actually applying them. Effective career planning, along with decision making, requires you to evaluate the predictions with the idea that economic conditions frequently change. That is, poor employment conditions in some fields and parts of the country today may well improve six months from now.

[13]O'Toole, "Finding Work," 67–68.

By reading daily newspapers, for example, *The Wall Street Journal* or *The New York Times*, you can learn about economic conditions and employment patterns. Financial and business sections of the paper often feature stories on business growth and industrial expansion in certain locations. The employment section may give you some idea of hiring trends.

Reading weekly and monthly magazines — *Business Week, Time, Forbes, Newsweek, Fortune*—should also be a part of your career exploration. Seek out articles which highlight various businesses and industries. Such articles will provide you with an idea of what is happening across the country.

In conclusion, career exploration is an invaluable process in decision making. As you explore, quite possibly you may discover that your qualifications do not measure up to the standards for a particular career; however, you should not necessarily abandon the career. If some of your qualifications are weak, you may be able to make up for them by possessing other strengths. If you lack several qualities prerequisite for success in a career, consider other career options before moving ahead with your work plans.

POINTS TO REVIEW

1. Exploring career classification systems may help you discover additional careers of interest.

2. You need to consider work adjustment and job satisfaction as you plan your lifelong career.

3. You should obtain both extensive and accurate information about careers when exploring them.

4. An important part of your career decision will be whether you find the actual work tasks in a career appealing.

5. The relationship between your personality and the requirements of a particular career may determine if you will feel satisfied, as well as attain success, as you perform the work.

6. You might list personal requirements of your preferred career to determine which requirements are most like your abilities and skills.

7. Meeting the required intellectual prerequisites of any career will contribute greatly to career adjustment and satisfaction.

8. Many states in the United States have laws requiring you to attain a license or certificate, beyond your educational training, in order to qualify for practice in a chosen career.

9. You and the marketplace change over time. As you explore career fields which interest you, consider those fields which may enable you to switch from one career to another.

10. You should study various careers having the idea that you want to move up the career ladder; that is, identify and evaluate career paths which offer upward career movement.

11. You should consider work conditions as you study careers.

12. The demand for workers is greatly influenced by the general condition of the national economy, technological development, legislative decisions, and change within the population.

13. Level of possible income is a factor to explore as you study preferred careers.

14. You can obtain sources of information about careers from libraries and counselors.

Experiential Exercises

Read and consider the following two situations.

1. Sandra, forty-eight years old, became a widow last year after her husband died in an automobile accident. Her only living relatives are two grown sons and their families. Although Sandra had sufficient income, she became bored staying at home and decided hastily to secure work, which might keep her busy. After working at a local hotel as a desk clerk, she finds herself not liking the working hours, the constant contact with strangers, the low pay, and the lack of creativity.

   a. How would you describe Sandra's situation?

   b. What do you suspect may be the cause of Sandra's feelings?

   c. How might Sandra have better approached her situation?

2. Elliot, a twenty-seven year old college graduate, with straight A grades in stationary engineering, left school four years ago. He has moved from as many as five different work settings. Elliot argues that he enjoys the stationary engineering, but his positions just don't work out. He is frequently absent, often comes to work late, has a negative attitude toward others, and demonstrates inconsistent work habits while on the job.

   a. How would you describe Elliot's situation?

    b. What seems to be the relationship between Elliot and his work environment?

    c. List factors which may be interfering with Elliot's career satisfaction.

    d. What might Elliot have to do to overcome his dissatisfaction?

3. Think about your ideal work environment. Would you rather work in a large urban area, a suburb, or a rural area? Inside, outside, or both? In what part of the United States would you prefer to work? What type of climate would you prefer?

    a. Rank order (list the most important to the least important) those factors you would prefer in your work environment.

        1.

        2.

        3.

    b. List as many careers as possible which might fulfill each of your three preferred factors stated in *a*.

c. After thinking about your interests, personal and work values, life-style, skills, and abilities, list below those careers from *b* which you would like to explore.

4. For each choice you listed in *3c,* try to answer the following questions.
   a. What work tasks are performed in this career?

   b. What personality requirements best suit this career?

   c. What intellectual abilities are necessary to perform this career?

   d. What education and/or training does this career require? How might I attain appropriate education and training?

   e. What steps do I take to enter this career?

    f. What opportunities are there to switch to other types of work within this field?

    g. How great are the possibilities for making vertical career moves within this field?

    h. Will I enjoy the working conditions for this career?

    i. In what locations are the most promising positions for this career?

    j. What kind of earnings can I expect if I work in this field?

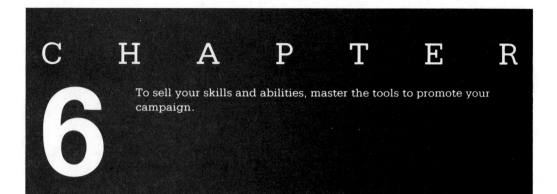

C H A P T E R

6

To sell your skills and abilities, master the tools to promote your campaign.

Organizing Your Career Campaign

A career campaign is similar to a political campaign. To win either one, you must have a plan of action. To win a career campaign, you should know your goals and have learned the essential tools for action—resumé, employment application, cover letter, placement folder, interview process, and follow-up letter. You will need to use step-by-step methods to market your skills and services to potential employers. Many individuals seeking employment are unsuccessful because they do not know how to use these tools effectively.

As stated in Chapter 5, before contacting potential employers, determine whether your interests and lifestyle are similar to your employment leads. As you contact promising career leads, promote yourself forcefully. But, promoting yourself requires you to know your career goals and skills. The point is, if you are not aware of your employable skills, no one else can learn about them through you. Once you have analyzed your skills and their relationship to potential employment leads, you must communicate your skills and services to prospective employers. This chapter discusses identifying your skills and using tools to communicate this information to a potential employer.

Larry Hamill

Your skills will be tested in your job search.

YOUR EMPLOYABLE SKILLS

Some people declare that they have few or no employable skills and abilities. Probably, these individuals have not taken the time to review their aptitudes, accomplishments, or achievements. A middle-aged woman, who wants to enter the career market after being a wife and raising a family, asks herself if she has any marketable skills. By examining her experiences as a homemaker and a mother, she will find that she has succeeded as an organizer, planner, budgeter, manager, and interior decorator. Take the time to evaluate your accomplishments, and you will find that you have considerable achievements and abilities. Then take a bit more time and consider which skills you used to reach these accomplishments.

Tips for Self-Assessment

- **What kinds of skills do I have that would lead to potential employment?**
- **How can I apply my personal skills in the career market?**

Many personal skills can be useful in various work settings. These skills are transferable—skills which you can move from one career to another. Three broad categories—*functional, adaptive,* and *specific or technical*—describe many careers.

FUNCTIONAL SKILLS

You can demonstrate functional skills as you move from one career to another. Functional skills allow you to deal with things, ideas, and people, or some combination of the three. A few functional skills are as follows:

Assigning tasks in ways which show respect for another individual and acceptance of her ideas

Developing and organizing programs

Obtaining information from people when they are sometimes unwilling to provide it or when they experience difficulty finding it

Creating various solutions to a problem when more than a single answer is possible

Locating resource materials necessary to solve a problem

ADAPTIVE SKILLS

Your adaptive skills are associated with a particular work setting, including your fellow workers within that setting. Adaptive skills are the general ways you adjust to the physical, interpersonal, and organizational conditions of your work setting. Adaptive skills allow you to cooperate with other workers and deal with a variety of situations, such as a supervisor's suggestions, peak and low sales periods, the noise or weather conditions associated with work tasks, change in managers/supervisors, changes of career tasks and/or functions, or changes in work schedule (rotating shifts). Adaptive skills used in one work setting may be transferred to another. Several examples of adaptive skills follow:

Adjusting to financial decisions in critical situations

Anticipating consumer needs

Working with a variety of people

Remaining flexible to organizational change

SPECIFIC OR TECHNICAL SKILLS

Having technical or specific skills can help you perform a specific task, when the job requires following an employer's specifications or requirements. Specific or technical skills, unlike functional and adaptive skills, are only transferable when specific work tasks in one career are the same as in another. The following are examples of specific or technical skills:

Preparing income taxes	Reading a blueprint
Handling a divorce case	Filling teeth
Driving a military tank	Filling a prescription
Repairing the body of an automobile	Adjusting damages to an automobile
Programming a computer	Selling property

Tips for Self-Assessment

- What are my functional, adaptive, and specific or technical skills?
- Which of these skills seems stronger than the others?
- How might I improve my functional or adaptive skills?

Identifying employable skills normally occurs during a career search, but determining the relationship of skills to potential employment is not enough. Instead, you should evaluate your skills and services as they relate to leads. When you know exactly what services and skills you have to offer, then you can make your strongest pitch to a potential employer. To succeed in the career market, you must know your product (skills and services) *and* potential employers who want to buy. You make known your skills and services through your employment applications, resumés, cover letters, placement folders, interviews, and follow-up letters.

EMPLOYMENT APPLICATION

Tips for Self-Assessment

- What do I know about myself that would be interesting or important to a potential employer?
- How personal should I be in responding to a potential employer's questions on an application?

The employment application asks a set of questions about the person applying for a position. Employers are moving toward the use of resumés, but many people hiring continue to require applicants to complete an application blank. This form summarizes information about an applicant which most interests the employer. An employer uses the application, or the resumé, to screen persons applying for a vacant position. Unlike the resumé, the employment application asks for specific information pertaining to the applicant with little, if any, opportunity for you, the applicant, to stress the strength of your skills and qualifications. If you are an older worker, a woman returning to work, a physically disabled person, or a veteran, you may have a limited opportunity to present your abilities and skills. Figure 6–1 (see facing pages 116–117) is an example of an employment application.

Employment applications vary only slightly from one to another, depending on the type of business or position available. Use the following suggestions for completing an application:

Be neat in completing the application.

Print clearly or type the requested information on the application.

Do not cross out responses.

Give truthful reasons for leaving earlier employment, but use acceptable ones, such as a desire for higher pay, an opportunity to continue or complete education, a furlough (or temporary lay off), a change in career goals, or a resignation agreed upon between employer and yourself.

Provide names and addresses of references who may influence the employer's decision to hire you (for example, ministers, instructors, or supervisors).

You should be cautious when filling out an application since it may not be advantageous to answer all the questions. Many questions of a personal nature are not permitted by law, either on an employment application or in an interview. Yet many employers still use applications asking for personal information. Such questions are illegal, unless the answers to the questions have a direct relation to the work being performed. Note that you have legal rights against such questions when seeking employment. Several laws protect you from providing information to questions about sex, ethnicity (or race), date of birth, weight, height, marital status, number of dependents and children, dates of school attendance, mental or physical disabilities, police arrests, or incarceration (imprisonment). Keep in mind that questions, which explore areas such as the ones just listed, can be asked only if they are related to the position for which you are applying.

RESUMÉ

A resumé should be a personally-designed, written summary of your education and experience, which will communicate your fitness for a particular position. Simply stated, your resumé sketches the skills and services you can offer a potential employer. You should know how to use this tool in your career campaign.

Application for Employment

DATE _____

Name _____ SS # _____
       (Last)   (First)   (Middle)

Present address _____ Telephone # _____
                Street Address   City

Phone where you can be reached if not at above number   Telephone # _____

Are there any periods during the year when you will not be available for work? Yes _____ No _____ When? _____

What is the earliest date you will be available to start work? _____

Are you licensed or certified by any trade or profession? Yes _____ No _____ Kind of license? _____

Have you worked for the Pirtle Space Corporation before?
Yes _____ No _____ When? _____

How did you hear of employment opportunities at Pirtle Corporation?

_____ Self-referral

_____ Advertisement

_____ Friend or relative

_____ Employment agency

_____ Other

Position Desired: First preference will be given first consideration

1. _____

2. _____

3. _____

Is there a minimum salary acceptable? Yes __ No __ If yes, what amount? _____

How long do you wish employment?
Years ____   Months ____

I will accept:
Full-time ____ Part-time ____ Temporary ____
                                (6 mos. or less)

If part-time, what hours can you work? _____
_____
_____

How do you feel you are qualified for the position(s) applied for?

_____

_____

_____

EDUCATION: List in order the educational institutions you have attended if applicable.

Dates From	To	Name of Institution	Major & Minor Courses Pursued	Degree or Certificate
High School				
College or Univ.				
Vocational, Technical or Trade Schools				

May we contact your present employer for references? _____

Employer _____ Address _____
(Present or Most Recent)   Street   City   State

Phone _____

Name and title of supervisor _____
From
Month _____ Year _____
From
Your job and description of duties _____
Month _____ Year _____

_____
Pay $ _____ Per _____

Reason for terminating this employment _____

Employer _____ Address _____
(Present or Most Recent)   Street   City   State

Phone _____

From
Name and title of supervisor _____
Month _____ Year _____
From
Your job and description of duties _____
Month _____ Year _____

_____
Pay $ _____ Per _____

Reason for terminating this employment _____

Employer _____ Address _____
(Present or Most Recent)   Street   City   State

Phone _____

From
Name and title of supervisor _____
Month _____ Year _____
From
Your job and description of duties _____
Month _____ Year _____

_____
Pay $ _____ Per _____

Reason for terminating this employment _____

REFERENCES

1. _____
   Name   Address   Phone

2. _____
   Name   Address   Phone

3. _____
   Name   Address   Phone

4. _____
   Name   Address   Phone

5. _____
   Name   Address   Phone

The above information is requested to become acquainted with your qualifications and IS NOT an offer of employment.

I certify that all of the information stated in this application is true to the best of my knowledge and belief, and I authorize you to refer to any former employers or others to verify the statements made.

_____

EQUAL OPPORTUNITY EMPLOYER   Signature

Tips for Self-Assessment

- What personal strengths do I want to communicate to a potential employer?
- What work and educational experiences have I had?
- How would I best describe my work achievements in a resumé?

Since many individuals are seeking work, personnel officials use resumés to select the best qualified or potentially dynamic workers. Generally, the resumé is the first step in employment selection. This statement should not be taken lightly. You design your resumé hoping it will convince a potential employer to give you an interview. Resumés should be effective—capable of selling your skills and services. As stated earlier, your resumé communicates who you are, including what skills you have to offer an employer.

Unlike an employment (or job) application, your resumé gives you more control over what you communicate to the person doing the hiring. You have the power to guide the employer's attention to those factors which market your most important products—your skills and services!

GUIDELINES FOR DEVELOPING A RESUMÉ

What do employers look for in a resumé? The answer seems easy. Employers screen your resumé to determine if you are an appropriate applicant. They decide which resumés to select from a mountain of resumés and then interpret the information communicated on them. Recognize that employers evaluate some areas on a resumé more critically than others based on the type of position they wish to fill.

Before developing a resumé, note the following guidelines regarding its appearance and its presentation of your experience, education, and accomplishments. The greater the accuracy with which you present your skills, the greater the chances an employer will decide to interview you.

Appearance of the Resumé   Many employers first evaluate resumés only by physical appearance. A carelessly typed, dog-eared resumé on onionskin or erasable bond paper may suggest undesirable traits to a potential employer. Even though you have outstanding qualifications, your resumé, if presented in this way, will communicate carelessness, untidiness, lack of organization, and an unprofessional attitude. On the other hand, an employer will usually read a resumé typed neatly on good quality paper, without visible corrections. Avoid the other extreme of presenting a glamorous resumé, with fancy borders or expensive typesetting. An employer may see such a resumé and wonder what you are attempting to hide!

Remember that your resumé is a brief sketch of your skills and services, not an in-depth history. Most employers have neither the time nor the urge to read through numerous pages.

Considering today's intense competition for career openings, employers look critically at each applicant. Your resumé should be long enough to sell your skills and services for employment, without being windy. While many experts in career planning suggest applicants submit one- to three-page resumés, consider writing a longer resumé, if you are in a technical field or have broad experiences. Short resumés, which do not describe complex career experiences, are no longer appropriate. A too-short resumé, only outlining your background, will not present a fair picture of your accomplishments and capabilities.

Your Experience or Work History   As an employer reads the section of a resumé labeled experience or employment history, he wants to learn when you began and ended each of your positions. You should give special attention to the method of presenting this information. Avoid leaving time gaps, suggesting that you are a "career hopper." If you have been out of work for several months, include your years in a position instead of the month and year you finished work. Some individuals unemployed for more than a year might choose to disregard the use of sequential listing by years and include the number of years they held a position rather than the exact year it began or ended.

Yet, it may be beneficial for you to focus on a rapid succession of careers which can suggest to an employer that you are a rising achiever with strong personal motivation. If your moves occurred as a result of a promotion, provide this information under each career description with a statement such as, "promotion based performance."

Another way for you to approach the experience section of the resumé is to present yourself as a well-rounded professional with a variety of skills to offer. While you are focusing on a specific area, you might present yourself as a skilled generalist through descriptions of other work responsibilities, as an applicant did in the following portion of her resumé.

> Additional (related but less important) duties include: supervising and training staff; working with insurance specialists in claim adjustments; preparing monthly and quarterly financial statements; assisting outside insurance agents with fiscal year audit.

Strive to make your resumé information sharp, focused, pertinent to the position you want. When you have stated a general career objective, focus your cover letter on a specific position, thus attracting the employer's attention to those factors of your resumé which deal with the specific requirements of the position vacancy.

Educational Background   Generally, you place educational background information immediately following your work experience profile. For some careers, particularly executive careers, educational information may or may not be significantly related to the position that you are seeking. Many employers will examine this section to determine your personal character or personality—your leadership ability or extracurricular activities. The position, for instance, of a travel agent or a human relations specialist would require an applicant to have an outgoing personal character and a desire to deal with people. An employer would view the education of an experienced applicant only as additional information about his career experience unless a definite type of education or degree were needed.

Work Accomplishments   As part of a successful career strategy, an effective resumé does not include shyness and modesty. It does give serious consideration to experiences and accomplishments which support your objectives. An employer will closely examine your work experience to identify skills or personal abilities which enabled you to complete your past accomplishments. A potential employer will be less interested in *what* you did than *how* you made something happen—how you controlled the action—as opposed to someone else causing it.

Before responding to an employment lead, you might first determine what you need to learn about the position and the company and then focus your resumé and cover letter (cover letter is discussed later in the chapter) on those questions. For example, does the position require a variety of talents? Is the ability to perform different tasks important, or will the tasks be specific? If you are responding to a lead from a small- or middle-sized company, it may be necessary for you to discover the various talents the position will require.

An interviewer has a picture in her mind about what qualifications are necessary in a position. It is up to you to penetrate that description in your resumé. For example, Grace is presenting herself as a generalist in merchandise marketing, while hunting for a career with a middle-sized company. She should also present hands-on experience in areas other than marketing. If you are seeking employment with a large business, you can give more effort to presenting details of your specialized skills. For instance, a company interviewer with a large, well-known electrical engineering firm probably would not be impressed by a variety of skills in several areas. This interviewer would examine a summation of strengths related to one or two skills.

Statements such as "highly energetic" or "effective interpersonal skills" may be appropriate for a position that specifically requires these skills; however, these types of statements are usually used by entry level applicants with little or no professional background to market to employers.

You need to support your accomplishments with your skills and professional involvements. Consider presenting solid professional achievements instead of a personalized statement.

Other Factors to Consider   Current resumé suggestions may help you present only useful and necessary information for marketing yourself. Consider the following as you develop your resumé.

1. *Photograph*—Generally, do not include a photograph with your resumé. New state and federal laws state that background and

professional qualifications should be the only factors used by an employer for employment consideration.

2. *Personal Information*—You are not required to list your ethnic background, marital status, age, height, weight, or health on the resumé. If you are a woman, you might care to omit that you are married since some employers believe that as a married woman, you may work only to assist your husband's career needs.

3. *Salary History and Requirements*—The appropriate place for presenting salary, bonus, or compensation is generally during the interview.

4. *Professional References*—You should expect the employer to have access to your references. Names and addresses of references are not usually listed on the resumé. You may consider stating, "References are available upon request." An employer is not likely to contact your references until you are seriously considered for a position.

Writing an effective resumé requires your time and effort, so you should prepare the resumé as soon as possible during the career search. After you write a trial copy of the resumé, ask a person who writes well to read your trial copy and offer any helpful suggestions to improve it. Personnel at a college or university career placement office may read the resumé and give you suggestions. Next, consider what you should include in your resumé to highlight your qualifications for employment.

RESUMÉ CONTENT

Follow general guidelines as you develop your resumé. To assist the employer in locating specific information, the resumé should be well organized, having separate sections containing background information, qualifications, and adequate spacing for neatness. Write your resumé so that your career skills, abilities, and other important information stand out. You should include the following items and clearly organize them.

Identifying Information   List your name and current address (both present and permanent), including zip code and telephone number.

Career Objectives   Your career objectives are the responsibilities, challenges, and work activities which you plan to undertake. The objectives should state the specific type of position you are seeking and imply your skills and abilities to the employer. Your career objectives need to be well-defined. You might want to include long-range goals as indications of your potential. An employer will want to know that you have thought about your career goals. Should you have more than one career interest, you might consider preparing a different resumé for each objective. If two companies have slightly differing openings for a computer programmer, you might tailor your career objective, on separate resumés, to the specific needs of each. Employers sometimes are less willing to hire you when your objectives appear unclear or too broad to meet the purpose of a career opening. If you are seeking a specific position which you know is available, be certain to state your objectives so they directly relate to that position.

Educational Background   If you have had previous work experiences which are closely linked to your career objectives, state them before *Educational Background*, and only state your higher education background. This section should include a brief summary of education and achievements. List your highest or most recent degree first and work backwards. Include all schools attended beyond high school and any training important to your career objectives. State the degree types and/or certificates which you have earned and the year you graduated or expect to graduate. List your grade point average, if you feel it is worth attention (if it is above a *B* or 3.00 average), scholarship honors, awards, or recognitions, but do not include details. (If you need to describe an award in detail, it probably does not belong in your resumé.) List any professionally-related training or special licenses in this section. Avoid mentioning workshops and seminars. This section should be brief, having no more than four to six lines.

Experience or Employment History   This section summarizes your work experiences and accomplishments, beginning with your present or most recent experience. Generally, information in this section includes:

1. Date of employment
2. Name and address of employer and nature of company or business
3. Position held
4. Specific career duties
5. Focus of responsibilities
6. Accomplishments

The employment history presents kinds of work you have done and may include your career titles or positions. Include your work experiences, which relate to the position for which you are applying or relate to your career objectives. For example, include full- and part-time work, volunteer work, student teaching, internships, and practicums.

If you are a recent college graduate or plan to graduate soon, do not be overly concerned of your lack of work experience directly related to your career objective. Many others are in your same position. What can you do about a lack of career experience? Think about the skills and abilities you have developed through work, school, or leisure-time activities which you might apply to other work settings. An employer evaluates your potential by focusing on skills and abilities which you can transfer to a company position. You might consider including these skills. Remember that an employer is more interested in *how* you have accomplished tasks, rather than *where* or *what* you have done. Employers seek potential workers who will take responsibility, engage in creative thinking, and make sound, effective decisions. So, you should stress your accomplishments in this section. Note the following example:

Experience:	JBD Corporation—Oklahoma City, Oklahoma
1983–present	*SENIOR ACCOUNTANT* Responsible for establishing, implementing, and maintaining all accounting controls. Prepared tax returns, monthly and quarterly financial statements, and budgets. Supervised 3 accountants and support staff. Reported directly to Department Chief.
Accomplishments:	. . . developed corporate accounts payable system designed to handle more than 12½ million in supplier payments. . . . recruited by CBE Corporation due to outstanding performance.

Accomplishments Related to Career or Career Objectives   If you are a student who lacks work experience, you may choose to list your strengths, experiences, and functional and adaptive skills in this section. You might list volunteer activities, knowledge of a foreign language, or other special abilities.

Military Experience (if applicable)   You should list your military branch and length of service, major duties, assignments, rank, and type of discharge. Relate your accomplishments during military service to the requirements and functions of your career objectives.

Activities and Interests   Provide a potential employer with a well-developed portrait of your *total self,* by describing your professional and community activities, club associations, hobbies, and other interests. If you have limited employment experience, you may choose to highlight your extracurricular activities. Include activities which indicate leadership ability, interpersonal skills, or show that you are a hard worker or self-starter. Try to be specific in your statements.

References   You do not need to include your references on the resumé. The only statement needed under this section is "References are available upon request." Be prepared to present your references to the employer during the interview. Take a typed list of three to five references. (Each reference should include previous employers, instructors, and persons employed in your chosen career field.) Also, carry a copy of your most recent transcript, in case the interviewer requests it. If you chose to list your references on the resumé, include the name, position, and address of each reference.

TWO TYPES OF RESUMÉS

Consider two of the most common resumés used by career seekers—the *reverse chronological sequence resumé* and the *functional resumé*. The chronological resumé begins with your most recent work and educational experiences and moves backward to the next most recent, as in the following example:

WORK EXPERIENCE

1984–Present	Casual Campus Shop Iowa City, Iowa
POSITION:	Sales Supervisor
DUTIES:	Responsible for all sales and displays of women's wearing apparel. Ordered materials required for showroom displays, trained beginning sales clerks and display personnel, and was awarded outstanding display showroom plaque.
1982–1984	Chisolm & Chisolm Department Store Iowa City, Iowa
POSITION:	Sales Clerk
DUTIES:	Worked directly with customers interested in men's clothing. Thorough knowledge of men's department merchandise and current fashion trends. Promoted to general sales supervision.

EDUCATION:

September 1984 to Present	Currently working on a Bachelor of Science degree in marketing at the University of Iowa. Degree to be completed by May, 1986.
1982–1984	Iowa City Junior College; Iowa City, Iowa. Associate degree in secretarial studies.

Recent college graduates with little work experience generally use the chronological resumé. It can also be an appropriate tool for more experienced workers with skills and training; however, a middle-aged career worker may see a disadvantage in this type of resumé because it stresses age and/or length of experience rather than skills and ability. If you feel that your professional background and skills will contribute to a position within a particular business, use this chronological form. Many employers will place little, if any, stress on dates. If you are not convinced you should date your work and educational experiences, consider the functional resumé.

Many employees consider the functional resumé the more useful. This type is effective if you have had many jobs, gaps in your employment history, dates which might work against you, volunteer experiences, or unrelated work experiences. The functional resumé is flexible. Use it to focus on your strengths, skills, and abilities within each work experience.

Rather than listing a sequential order of work experiences, simply indicate the number of years you have been employed in a position with a certain company. An older person, who fears his age may be viewed as a negative factor by the employer, can stress recent educational and career experiences.

Tips for Self-Assessment

- Why is a chronological resumé or a functional resumé better for me?
- To what extent should I rely solely on my own skills to write my resumé?

The functional resumé enables you to draw upon your functional and adaptive skills. From these skills, choose only those which relate to the position for which you are applying. Do not overlook previous professional and/or nonprofessional work experiences which can strengthen your employment potential for a position—your organizational skills, bookkeeping and financial reporting, telephone screening, or management of a small group of researchers. The following experience and education sections are from a functional resumé:

CAREER OBJECTIVE:	Position in business aspects of publishing field offering opportunities for advancement.
EXPERIENCE:	Worked 3 years for "The Bryan Mount Holley News" as a <u>business manager</u> . Responsible for financial management, advertising, and production. Directed staff of seven members. Qualified for this position through work during sophomore and junior years.
	<u>Office Assistant for Camp Evangeline, Naples, Maine</u>. Composed and typed letters for camp director, kept financial statements, prepared bills, and prepared checks for signature. Generally, served as administrative assistant to the director.
EDUCATION:	Bachelor's degree with an English major, economics minor, and foreign language coursework from Bryan Mount Holley College, Denton, Texas. Dale Carnegie coursework in public relations. Various seminars and workshops in business management and publishing.
REFERENCES:	Available upon request.

The functional resumé can be useful for various people seeking employment opportunities. These persons may be women returning to the marketplace, military veterans, entry (or beginning) level workers, persons with limited full-time work experience in a particular field, persons with career experience in different fields, older workers who fear their age may be a factor, college or university graduates with limited work experiences, or college and university graduates with a general educational program which lacks relationship to a specific form of work. If you need to emphasize your skills and abilities in order to obtain a position, seriously consider using the functional resumé.

STYLE AND APPEARANCE OF YOUR RESUMÉ

The writing style of your resumé should be accurate, to the point, well-organized, and brief. Use active verbs in the resumé such as *trained, developed, directed, managed, edited, supervised, coordinated,* or *designed.* Avoid using the word *I.* The employer reading your resumé will already know to whom you are referring. By avoiding the use of *I,* you become free to state your accomplishments without bragging. Try to use complete sentences, or use phrases, as long as their meaning is clear to a reader other than yourself. Avoid the use of slang, professional or trite expressions, and abbreviations. For correct word usage and correct spelling, use a dictionary as you review your resumé, or ask a person who is skilled in English usage to read your resumé.

Generally, the resumé should be one to three pages long. Again, your resumé should be as long as you need to market your skills, abilities, and qualifications. An experienced worker with advanced degrees or extensive training might need more space to present her work history and accomplishments than a person with no professional work experience or a recent college graduate.

Organize the spacing on each page so that the overall resumé is visually appealing. Allow one-inch margins on both sides and at the top and bottom of each page to give a neat appearance. Fill the page from top to bottom and avoid leaving unnecessary space without going into the margins. On draft copies, experiment with the arrangements of the headlines and captions to determine which style best compliments your skills and services. Avoid extra capital letters and underlining. Use these tools only when you need them, not when you want to improve your presentation of information.

Pick standard paper, size 8½ inches by 11 inches. Should you prefer a slightly different size, consider legal size or a sheet which opens easily having a booklet form. Many employers claim that resumés nonstandard in size create handling and storage difficulties. Choose high-quality paper, either white bond, off-white, gray, or beige. This latter color, beige, provides distinction without limiting the focus of your skills, services, or qualifications.

Use a photo-offset printing process for duplicating of your resumé. Another acceptable method, although expensive, is having your resumé printed. Avoid ditto copies, carbon copies, or photo reproduction copies of your resumé.

COVER LETTER

Tips for Self-Assessment

- How polished are my writing skills?
- How will I organize and write an effective cover letter to emphasize my strengths?
- What persons can I ask for assistance in preparing my cover letter?

When a potential employer receives your resumé, a cover letter should appear with it. This letter briefly introduces you and encourages an employer to read your resumé. The cover letter establishes the purpose behind your sending the resumé.

HOW TO PLAN A COVER LETTER

An effective cover letter is well focused and specifically designed for the position for which you are applying. You might develop a cover letter using the following suggestions:

1. Your cover letter should consist of not more than one page. Anything else that you would like to state about yourself should be saved for the appropriate time during the interview.
2. Although typed letters are preferable, you might use photocopying or photo-offset printing.
3. Basic content of the cover letter should include the following items:
   a. title or position for which you are applying
   b. your objective for the position for which you are applying
   c. your long-range career objectives
   d. your purpose for seeking the position
   e. your knowledge of the company or business

Before you develop your cover letter, keep in mind the following guidelines:

1. Try to determine who will be conducting the interview for the position. You might telephone the company or business to request this information.
2. Identify the person who will actually read your cover letter.
3. Show that you have the skills and services to fill the requirements of the position.
4. Give brief examples of your career accomplishments which directly relate to the position you seek.
5. Emphasize important points in the resumé which identify your skills and qualifications.

6. Communicate that you can meet the employer's needs for the position, without appearing to brag about your qualifications.
7. Be straightforward in your letter. Do not be longwinded or rambling.
8. Present yourself as a potential worker in the employer's company. So as to insure that you present a favorable impression, check the letter several times for correct spelling, word usage, and punctuation. You might ask an English teacher or instructor to read and correct it too.

PARTS OF THE COVER LETTER

Use the preceding guidelines to develop an effective cover letter. Use the following suggestions while writing the beginning, basic message, and closing of the letter.

Opening Paragraph   Gain the employer's attention by stating how and where you obtained information about the position. Give the name of the source (individual or ads) from which you learned of the position. In a single statement, tell how you will be an asset to the company.

Middle paragraph   Encourage the employer to speak with you. You might include several factors in the letter to attract the employer. Focus on skills or services which make you suited for the position. Emphasize any awards and recognitions that you have received. Present your accomplishments from former jobs. You might state how your skills and qualifications are related to the objectives of the position and how you would fill the responsibilities or duties of that position. If you do not have specific or required skills, use this section to present other adaptive and functional skills. If you have been out of work or are shifting careers, stress those skills and services which you can transfer to the new position. Do not forget to include your professional and non-professional experiences.

Closing   Request the employer to take action. You might ask for an interview and indicate that you will contact the office. For instance, "I will be contacting your office in a matter of three or four days to arrange for an appointment." Or, you may just request an interview, stating that you will be available at the employer's convenience. In this case, be sure to provide your telephone number and time you will be available to receive calls.

A suggested ending of the cover letter should include a complimentary closing, your written signature, and then your name type written. The format for this is as shown in the following example:

Complimentary closing (such as cordially)

Your signature above your typed name

Typed name

PREPARING A CAREER PLACEMENT FOLDER

Tips for Self-Assessment

- How can I arrange for my placement folder to be on file in the college placement office?
- Although I have my folder on file, what steps should I take to make sure that I do not lose any of my employment leads?

Your college placement counselor may help you develop your resumé and cover letters for employment opportunities. Since many potential employers require references and resumés, most university career placement centers encourage their seniors and graduates to develop a career package, including current resumé and letters of reference, to be forwarded to employers upon request. Once you have a current resumé and several letters of reference on file, this college placement office usually sends this information to potential employers during a career campaign. You may also request your placement office to forward your credentials to employers, should an employment advertisement or employer state that the credentials are necessary when applying for a specific position. Generally, you should update your resumé, personal information sheet, and letters of reference at least once a year, even after you are employed, because you will have new career opportunities and your career goals can change.

Keep in mind that you may not want to use the resumé and reference letters which are on file in the placement office because they may not fit the position for which you are applying. You may have to design other resumés, as well as reference letters, for the positions you seek. In short, arrange for your placement credentials to be on file with the college or university placement office, but be sure your resumé and reference letters are appropriate for the position you are seeking.

THE EMPLOYMENT INTERVIEW

Tips for Self-Assessment

- How threatening do I perceive an employment interview to be?
- How prepared am I for my employment interview?
- Is my appearance appropriate for this interview?
- What else am I communicating to the employment interviewer, other than the verbal messages I state?
- How well do I listen and respond to others?

Submitting an effective resumé and cover letter can lead to an employment interview. Many persons look upon this interview as a threat, fearing failure even before beginning the interview process. Much of this fear, and sometimes failure, occurs due to insufficient preparation for and understanding of the interview itself.

The interview is an exchange of information between you and the employer to determine whether a mutual interest exists. Interviewers do not intentionally threaten you by asking difficult questions. You should remember that most employers or interviewers are pleasant and helpful. They represent businesses which are concerned for developing good public relations.

The interview is the time three types of information are shared. First, the employer can gather necessary information about you which you have not covered in your resumé, employment application, or cover letter. Secondly, you can gain the information beyond that which is stated in the employer's printed material. Finally, a basis of communication between you and the place of employment can occur.

PREPARATION

Sound preparation may not only enable you to strengthen your interview performance, it also may help you build trust between you and the interviewer. By processing accurate information, you can develop reasonable expectations about the interview process; the arrangement, content, and length of interview; the role of and style of the interviewer; your role; the way hiring decisions are made; and your chances of getting a favorable

Generally, employment interviews are pleasant, open exchanges of information.

decision. In preparing, you learn what to say, which enables you to sell your skills and services more effectively. Spend several hours developing an effective sales approach, which will mesh your style of presentation with knowledge of your product—your skills and services. You might consider the following suggestions:

1. Be aware of a prospective business's financial condition, products or services, and major locations.
2. Be able to discuss your interest in working with the company or business.
3. Be prepared to ask at least three good questions related to the structure or organization of the business, its services or products, or policies of the business. Avoid those questions which are already answered in the company's literature.

Do not put yourself in an awkward position by asking the inverviewer unrelated questions. Focus your questions only on accurate information.

While preparing for an interview, you should also reexamine your strengths and be able to discuss your skills and abilities. This preparation should include the following:

1. Study your personal qualities, so that you will be able to understand and sell your skills and services.
2. Be ready to discuss in about three minutes your potential assets for the company.
3. Bring an updated resumé and open letter of reference to the interview, if the employer does not already have one.
4. Bring a pen and a note pad.
5. Practice using the interviewer's name and determine his or her role within the company or organization.
6. Practice a firm handshake.
7. Avoid chewing gum and smoking before entering and during the interview.
8. Arrive 10 to 15 minutes early at the place of the interview before the interview starts.

APPEARANCE

Assessing your appearance is another important part of your reexamination. The impression you first make on an employer or interviewer is based on your appearance. How you look can strongly influence the decision to hire you. Carefully check out your dress and grooming. Are you neat, clean? Are you wearing appropriate clothes for the position which you are seeking? To wear your typical high school or campus classroom clothes to a business interview would not make much sense. If you are seeking a white-collar position, leave casual clothes at home—dress like a business person. Avoid extremes in appearance (busy patterns, bold colors, roughly tailored styles, and current fads). No evidence exists that how you appear in the interview will affect your actual work performance; however, employers regard neatness, taste, and personal cleanliness as signs of your work habits.

Generally, men should wear business suits but should not wear ties which seem to *stand out.* Women should avoid excessive jewelry. Another important part of personal appearance is grooming. Manicured nails, appropriately styled hair, and shined shoes are all a must. Women should avoid heavy facial make-up and heady perfumes. In short, as you evaluate your personal appearance, including dress and grooming, be conservative.

COMMUNICATION SKILLS

How well you communicate during the interview can influence whether or not an interviewer will hire you. Sandra L. Terrell and Francis Terrell[1] found in their study that most personnel managers will give you less time in the interview if your speech is nonstandard English. Stated another way, those applicants who speak the language most similar to that of the interviewer, usually standard English, receive more time during the interview and are more frequently hired than those who use slang expressions, broken English, ethnic dialect, or have a heavy foreign accent. Since some interviewers have negative attitudes toward Black or Appalachian speech, it makes sense to try and use traditional English during the interview. Avoid using nonstandard English during the interview. The price can be costly.

While speaking well is important, being a good listener is equally necessary during the interview. Listen to what the interviewer is saying to you. Some studies indicate that within the interview, many interviewers talk about two-thirds of the time; whereas, the applicants talk only about one third of the time. If this is the case, you are at a disadvantage since you will have little opportunity to express your strengths and qualifications. Listening will help you to effectively respond to the interviewer's questions and use the interviewer's topic as an opportunity to make your necessary points.

Most successful candidates' language and delivery communicate an active, assertive style. Practice using clear, concrete language. Try to sound decisive by avoiding weak phrases such as "pretty good," "I guess," or "I feel." Use words which create active pictures, such as, *advantage, progress, achievement,* or *purpose.*

Avoid long, complicated sentences which may mean little to the listener. Use relatively short sentences, which are simple and connected with meaningful transitions. Your gestures and tone of voice can also express assertive behavior. Vary your speaking rate, force, volume, and pitch to show self-assurance. Try to avoid verbalizing pauses, for example, "uh," "like," "I mean," "you know," and old or worn out expressions. If the inverviewer cannot hear you as you answer questions, you may be suggesting that you lack the necessary energy and enthusiasm to be an effective worker. Indicate you are alert and self-confident by using direct

[1]Sandra L. Terrell and Francis Terrell, "Effects of Speaking Black English Upon Employment Opportunities." *(ASHA) American Speech-Language-Hearing Association* 25 (June, 1983): 27–29.

eye contact with the interviewer, actively listening to the interviewer's statements, leaning slightly forward, smiling at appropriate times, and using occasional head nods.

You can best demonstrate your active and assertive style by responding to the interviewer in a strong voice at a relatively rapid rate. Use complete, specific sentences, and eliminate slow, indirect, and ineffective speech.

What type of questions do interviewers ask during an employment interview? The *Northwestern Endicott Report* (1983), published by the Placement Center at Northwestern University, includes a survey of more than one hundred well-known businesses and industries regarding the employment of college graduates. From this survey, Northwestern University published sixty-seven of the most frequently asked questions by employment interviewers of college seniors during interviews as shown in Figure 6–2.

Studying these questions can help you prepare for similar interview questions. It should not be difficult to answer questions like the ones listed, providing you prepare for them before entering the interview. It is unlikely that a single interviewer will ask you all the questions. You should expect to be asked others; however, these questions give you some idea of what you are likely to face during the interview. But again, it is important for you to listen carefully to the interviewer to be able to respond effectively. Effective communication during the interview includes using both standard English and active listening skills. The outcome of your interview will depend greatly on how well you are prepared to answer the interviewer's questions.

STAGES OF THE INTERVIEW

Generally, an employment interview has five stages, an opening, a period for background information, discussion of the available position, closing remarks, and follow-up. Length of time for each stage will differ from one interview or interviewer to another. Although the fifth stage, follow-up, is very much a part of the interview, it occurs shortly after the actual interview. You should examine what happens in each of these stages.

Opening   During the first few moments of the interview, build a positive relationship with the interviewer. You and the interviewer may fill this stage with small talk to put you at ease and build the climate for the remaining stages. Perhaps you will find the interviewer doing most of the talking. Remember, the interviewer's first impressions can be her last impressions of you. The interviewer makes judgments about your looks, communication skills, manners, and eagerness. How you greet the interviewer—sit, talk, look, and shake her hand—play an important part in the impression you make in these first few minutes.

Call the interviewer by her name. For example, the interviewer might introduce herself as "Patricia Smith," rather than "Mrs." or "Ms. Smith." You

1. What are your future vocational plans?
2. In what school activities have you participated? Why? Which did you enjoy the most?
3. How do you spend your spare time? What are your hobbies?
4. In what type of position are you most interested?
5. Why do you think you might like to work for our company?
6. What jobs have you held? How were they obtained and why did you leave?
7. What courses did you like best? Least? Why?
8. Why did you choose your particular field of work?
9. What percentage of your college expense did you earn? Why?
10. How did you spend your vacations while in school?
11. What do you know about our company?
12. Do you feel that you have received a good general training?
13. What qualifications do you have that make you feel that you will be successful in your field?
14. What extracurricular offices have you held?
15. What are your ideas on salary?
16. How do you feel about your family?
17. How interested are you in sports?
18. If you were starting college all over again, what courses would you take?
19. Do you prefer any specific geographic location?
20. Do you date anyone regularly?
21. How much money do you hope to earn at age 30? 35?
22. Why did you decide to go to this particular school?
23. Do you think that your extracurricular activities were worth the time you devoted to them? Why?
24. What do you think determines a person's progress in a good company?
25. What personal characteristics are necessary for success in your chosen field?
26. Why do you think you would like this particular type of job?
27. What are your parents' occupations?
28. Tell me about your home life during the time you were growing up.
29. Do you prefer working with others or by yourself?
30. What kind of boss do you prefer?
31. Are you primarily interested in making money or do you feel that service to humanity is your prime concern?

FIGURE 6-2 **Questions frequently asked during the employment interview**

Reprinted by permission from *The Northwestern Endicott Report* published by the Northwestern University Placement Center, Evanston, Illinois 60201, 1983.

32. Can you take instructions without feeling upset?
33. Tell me a story!
34. Do you live with your parents? Which of your parents have had the most profound influence on you?
35. How did previous employers treat you?
36. What have you learned from some of the jobs you have held?
37. Can you get recommendations from previous employers?
38. What interests you about our product or service?
39. What was your record in military service?
40. Have you ever changed your major field of interest while in college? Why?
41. When did you choose your college major?
42. Do you feel you have done the best scholastic work of which you are capable?
43. How did you happen to go to college?
44. What do you know about opportunities in the field in which you are trained?
45. Have you ever had any difficulty getting along with students and faculty?
46. Which of your college years was the most difficult?
47. What is the source of your spending money?
48. Do you own any life insurance?
49. Have you saved any money?
50. Do you have any debts?
51. How old were you when you became self-supporting?
52. Did you enjoy your four years at this university?
53. Do you like routine work?
54. Do you like regular hours?
55. What size city do you prefer?
56. What is your major weakness?
57. Define cooperation!
58. Do you demand attention?
59. Do you have an analytical mind?
60. Are you eager to please?
61. What do you do to keep in good physical condition?
62. Have you had any serious illness or injury?
63. Are you willing to go where the company sends you?
64. What job in our company would you choose if you were entirely free to do so?
65. What types of books have you read?
66. Have you plans for graduate work?
67. What types of people seem to rub you the wrong way?

FIGURE 6-2 (continued)

then should address her as "Ms. Smith," unless told differently. Avoid greeting the interviewer by her first name or nickname, unless the interviewer has earlier encouraged you to use it.

Follow any clues the interviewer may give you. For instance, return a firm hand shake. If you are a woman, you can take the initiative, should you desire, to shake hands.

Briefly pause before taking a seat, to allow the interviewer to provide one and to show you where she would like for you to sit. Avoid smoking unless you have been invited or permission has been given.

Background Information   This second stage shifts from casual conversation to a higher level of communication. The interviewer's form of questioning will depend on whether the interview is structured or unstructured. In a structured interview, the interviewer will ask you to respond to a standard set of questions in a more or less prescribed order. In an unstructured interview, the interviewer will follow whatever pattern of questioning seems most appropriate. Interviewers representing large companies frequently conduct structured interviews. The interviewer is likely to ask direct questions which deal with your skills and qualifications and begin to evaluate whether or not you are suited for the company. The interviewer observes your verbal ability, your self-confidence, how you deal with others, your level of motivation about the position, your personal values, and whether there is a balance between your career goals and activities outside your course of study.

Perhaps, the interviewer may ask open-ended questions, such as, "What can you tell me about yourself?" "How did you become interested in this field?" "Why do you want to work for this company?" This stage of the interview provides you with opportunities to respond to *when, why,* or *where* questions related to your background. At this time you can discuss your work experiences which do not appear on your resumé and draw upon your transferable skills. You can emphasize your strengths and develop your skills and services. Avoid spending talking at length about yourself, as you attempt to make these last two points.

At some point the interviewer will present information about the company. You can take control of the interview by asking thoughtful questions to encourage the employer to do a great deal of talking. You will want to ask the interviewer some direct questions about company operations, policies, planning, and products or services. Examples of your questions might be the following: What are the major problems faced by this division of your company? What style of management prevails in this division or in the ABC company? What kind of orientation and in-service training can I expect the J. B. Smith Company to provide me as part of this position?

You are likely to be more successful if you actively participate in the employment interview. Develop a focused, optimistic presentation. Engage in an active role by presenting messages, rather than just sitting and being questioned. Show that you are energetic. You might consider asking the first questions to put relations between you and the interviewer on equal terms. Asking thoughtful, relevant questions allows you to take control and encourages the interviewer to do most of the talking. Your questions can permit you to demonstrate, rather than talk about, your abilities and to collect information about the company you might otherwise not obtain. You can sell yourself by asking pertinent questions, by listening carefully, and by introducing accomplishments at well-timed intervals during the exchange of information. During this stage of the interview, the interviewer is attempting to determine your qualifications and to match these with a particular position.

Discussion of Employment Opportunity The third stage starts once the interviewer believes that he recognizes your skills and services and you see a match between the company and yourself. At this point, you might make sure that the interviewer understands your career goals and objectives. The interviewer may discuss certain information about the company, such as its operations and activities. This information may trigger certain questions in your mind that you would like answered. You may ask these questions, but avoid starting a discussion about pay or salary until the interviewer brings up the topic and other benefits. Concentrate on the position first and salary second. Your bargaining power on salary will be stronger after the company has decided that you are the best choice.

Career specialists report successful employment applicants have referred to the company by name four times as often as unsuccessful applicants during an interview.[2] Use the name of the company as you state your career goals and throughout the interview.

Closing During this stage, the interviewer may provide you with information concerning the employment procedure. The interviewer might let you know when you may expect to hear from the company, schedule you for testing, have you complete an application, arrange for a later interview, or recommend a visit to the company. You should not expect to leave the interview with a firm employment offer. The interviewer may need to review your qualifications at a later date with other company personnel, before they can make a decision to hire you. You may ask if there will be another interview, and if so, when can you expect it. One such closing may include trial questions such as, "Could you give me an idea of how I stack up against other applicants for this position?" "Does my experience seem to be what you are looking for?"

Strive to end the interview on a positive note. You could tell the interviewer that you are more excited about the position now than before the interview. Tell the interviewer how much you enjoyed meeting her.

Follow-Up The day after the interview, send a brief follow-up letter to the interviewer thanking him for discussing the position with you. Here is a chance to let the interviewer know you are interested in the position and

[2]Judith L. Enns, "Gaining the Edge on Job Offers," *National Business Employment Weekly*, 3 July 1983, 5–6.

would like to be considered for it. Stress again your specific qualifications, or return the employment applications which the interviewer may have given to you. Return the application, regardless of what may have happened in the interview. Be sure to keep your follow-up letter short, and end it by stating that you are looking forward to hearing about the results of the position. Consider this sample follow-up letter.

> Dear Ms. Smith:
>
> Just a short note to thank you for discussing the vacancy in the Chemical Engineering Division with me yesterday. I enjoyed our talk and found your comments helpful in providing a clear picture of the organization and the expectations of the position.
>
> I am truly enthusiastic about the position that we discussed. I believe my experience as a chemical engineer with Westinghouse for the past three summers and my Master's degree in chemical engineering both would be solid preparations to meet the needs of the position.
>
> With this letter you will find my completed employment application. The Admissions Office at Oscar Rose State Engineering Institute is sending a copy of my transcript to you.
>
> I look forward to hearing from you soon. Thanks again for your time and encouragement.
>
> Sincerely yours,
>
> James S. Brown
>
> Enclosure

You will find out whether or not the position is yours, either by telephoning or writing a letter. The interviewer may show interest in you by calling for another interview, especially if you two have not decided on a salary agreement. A phone call from the interviewer is generally a positive sign, but it does not necessarily mean that you will be offered a position. The unpleasant news of an employment rejection can come by mail or by phone, and sometimes even after an applicant has been offered and accepted the position vacancy.

Tips for Self-Assessment

- **How well do I understand the stages of the employment interview?**
- **How prepared am I to handle possible employment rejections?**

NEGATIVE FACTORS OBSERVED BY INTERVIEWERS

Many employment applicants are unsuccessful because they failed to prepare for the interview or because they simply disregarded factors which were important to company interviewers. *The Northwestern Endicott Report* (1983) lists what the interviewers of large company consider to be negative behaviors during the interview, see Figure 6-3.

1. Poor or inappropriate personal appearance.
2. Passive or indifferent attitude.
3. Lack of tact, maturity, or vitality—ill mannered.
4. No knowledge about organization or position offered.
5. Lack of career planning—indecision.
6. No knowledge about organization or position offered.
7. Lack of eye contact.
8. Evasive or hedging answers to questions.
9. Late for interview.
10. Limp, fishy handshake.
11. Slippery resumé or application.
12. Poor expression, diction, or grammar.
13. Overbearing, overaggressive, or conceited.
14. Asked no questions about job or organization.
15. Lack of confidence and poise.
16. Over-emphasis on money.
17. Condemnation of past employers or school.
18. Unwillingness to relocate.
19. Reluctance to begin in an open position.
20. Wants a position only for short time.
21. Failure to participate in community activities.
22. Cynical, strong prejudices, or intolerance.
23. Narrow interests.
24. Inability to accept criticism.
25. High pressure tactics.

FIGURE 6–3   **Unnecessary reasons for interview failure**

Reprinted by permission from the *Northwestern Endicott Report*, published by the Northwestern University Placement Center, Northwestern University, Evanston, Illinois 60201, 1983.

Give serious consideration to these factors before entering an interview. By following the suggested steps stated earlier, you may leave the interview as a winner.

PREPARING FOR POSSIBLE EMPLOYMENT REJECTION

Just because an interviewer grants you an interview, does not mean that he will offer you a position. In spite of good preparation, most applicants will face rejection at some point within their career search. Prepare yourself for coping with rejection. Not being offered a position can make you feel depressed, reduce your motivation, and contribute to feelings of low self-worth.

What can you do to prepare for rejection? First, realize that employment rejection is common. Not receiving an offer is something which happens because there are so many persons seeking employment. Enter your career search with the idea, "If I am not offered a position with one employer, that just increases my possibilities for success with the next one." This attitude will help you continue your efforts to achieve career goals. Call potential employers at various times to find out about present employment opportunities. Sometimes career vacancies can occur sporadically.

In certain situations, your sex or ethnic group can be either an advantage or disadvantage. Legal procedures are available, if you are not offered a position for these reasons, but the legal procedures may offer little help during an ongoing career search. Therefore, you should be prepared to deal with these discriminatory situations, if they happen to you. Also, you may consider becoming part of a support group of persons who are seeking employment and experiencing rejection. This type of group may help you share career search techniques and ways to handle employment rejection.

Employment rejection need not be something that overly concerns you. Awareness of sources of information about potential employers, career leads, and working conditions can lead to successful employment rather than employment rejection. Knowing how to research employment sources can help you obtain a desired position.

POINTS TO REVIEW

1. Career-related skills can be placed in three broad groups—functional, adaptive, and specific or technical.
2. Functional and adaptive skills can be transferred from one career to another.
3. Winning the career campaign may depend upon how well you use the necessary tools—empoyment application, resumé, cover letter, career placement folder, interview, and follow-up letter.
4. Employers look for specific information in a resumé—appearance, work experience or history, academic background, and work accomplishments.
5. Seriously consider the following factors before including them on your resumé: photograph, personal information, salary requirements, and references.
6. A resumé's content includes identifying information, career objectives, experience or work history, and references.
7. Two types of resumés are the chronological and functional. The functional resumé is considered the most useful by many employers.
8. Effective preparation for the employment interview includes checking out your personal appearance, using good English, adopting an assertive style of communication, and recognizing possibilities of success in all interviews.
9. The interview generally contains five stages—opening, background information, discussion of career opportunities, closing, and follow-up.

Experiential Exercises

1. One way you can identify possible transferable work skills is to consider the organizations (civic, social, political, community, or academic) with which you have been involved and the kinds of responsibilities you had with each. Below, give the name of the organization and describe how you were involved.

   Organization   *Responsibilities and/or Duties*

2. Another way to identify your transferable skills is to look at hobbies or pastimes you may have had. List each of your hobbies or pastimes and skills you developed while enjoying them.

   Hobbies   *Skills*

3. Looking back at questions *1* and *2*, which of your organizational responsibilities or duties and hobby skills can you use in a career? Beside each responsibility or skill, list a corresponding work requirement found in the marketplace.

   Responsibilities or Skills   *Possible Work Requirements*

4. The employment application blank is one important tool in your career campaign. Some employers still ask questions on such an application which are illegal and may work against you. Carefully examine the application blank shown on the following pages (143–44), and

   a. List those items from the application which are illegal for employers to ask.

     1.

     2.

     3.

     4.

     5.

     6.

     7.

     8.

     9.

     10.

   b. Refer to items you listed in *a*, and give a reason why each is considered illegal.

     1.

     2.

     3.

     4.

     5.

     6.

     7.

     8.

Employment Application Blank

Date _____

PERSONAL DATA

Name _____

Present address _____
             No.   Street

City _____

State _____ Zip code

Height _____

Date of birth _____

Weight _____

U.S. Citizenship   Yes _____   No _____

If no, specify country _____

Do you own your own home?

       Yes _____   No _____

Disabilities if any _____

Social Security number _____

Telephone number _____

Sex _____

Race _____

Marital status   Single _____

                       Married _____

                       Divorced _____

                    Separated _____

                      Widowed _____

Number of dependents _____

Number of children _____

PAST EMPLOYMENT

List all of the jobs you have held beginning with your most recent.

Employer and address	Dates of employment	Describe the work you did	Job title	Last weekly salary	Reason for leaving

EDUCATIONAL HISTORY

School	Name and address of school	Dates attended	Program of study	Did you graduate?	List degrees
Elementary				___ Yes ___ No	
High school				___ Yes ___ No	
College				___ Yes ___ No	
Other				___ Yes ___ No	

MILITARY SERVICE

Have you served in the military? ___ Yes ___ No   Dates of service _____

What branch? _____   Rank/Rate at discharge _____

Describe your duties or MOS _____

PERSONAL REFERENCES

Do not use relatives or employers.

Name	Address	Position	Telephone

POSITION APPLIED FOR

Position(s) applied for _____

Expected salary _____   Have you previously
                                    been employed with us? ___ Yes ___ No

Dates you can start work _____   If so, when? _____

Whom may we notify in case of emergency, if we should hire you? _____

_____
Street   City   State   Telephone

_____
Signature of applicant

- -

(For office use only)

Interviewer _____

9.

10.

5. Look back at your past work experience (volunteer, military, and community services) or professional memberships, and consider *what* you accomplished during each experience and *how* you accomplished it. List your work or related activities and your accomplishments below.

Work or Related Activities   *Accomplishments*

1.

2.

3.

4.

5.

6.

7.

8.

9.

10.

6. Practice writing each of the following sections of a resumé. Later, you can organize them into a draft of your resumé.

Career Objectives

Experience or Employment History (include accomplishments)

Special Skills and Services

Honors and Awards

Career Interests

Memberships

7. Decide whether you will prepare a *chronological* or *functional* resumé. Then, using your answers from question *6,* write the rough draft of your resumé on a separate sheet of paper.

8. The following exercise lists items which are related to assertive behavior. After each statement, place a check mark in the appropriate box to rate your assertiveness.

Behaviors	Yes	Sometimes	No
1. I usually take control of the conversation.			
2. I'm usually straightforward in what I have to say.			
3. Frankly, people generally take advantage of me.			
4. I enjoy initiating conversations with strangers whom I have known only for a short time.			
5. I prefer to take a relaxed attitude.			
6. There are times when I just cannot speak up before others.			
7. I'm open and frank about my feelings.			
8. Most people seem to be more aggressive and assertive than I am.			
9. When I have done something worthwhile, I usually let others know it.			
10. I find it difficult to say *no* to others.			
11. I usually know what to say when I am given a compliment.			
12. I'm quick to tell you what I think.			
13. I would prefer applying for a position by writing letters rather than by being interviewed.			
14. I usually don't hesitate to ask questions.			

Look over how you rated your behaviors and list the ones which you feel need improvement.

9. Assume that the following questions are being asked of you during an employment interview. After each question, write your response.

   a. How would you describe yourself?

   b. What kinds of experiences have you had?

   c. How do you think your college experience has prepared you for a position with this company?

   d. What do you know about our company?

   e. How would you describe your strengths and weaknesses?

   f. What do you see yourself doing five years from now?

   g. What would you like to say about yourself?

   h. Are there any questions you would like to ask me?

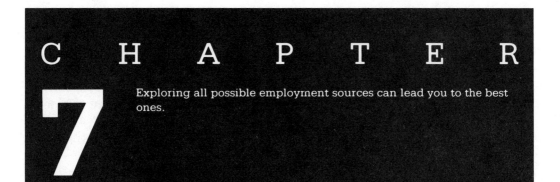

C H A P T E R

7

Exploring all possible employment sources can lead you to the best ones.

Researching Employment Opportunities

After you learn what career field interests you, how to attain the educational training for that career, and how to communicate with potential employers, your next step is to learn where to find employment leads. Over the years employment has become difficult to obtain in many fields. Energetic hopefuls with high expectations, along with less eager persons with low expectations, have saturated the marketplace. Most openings have many applicants vying for them. Many college graduates, others looking for work for the first time, and those switching careers during middle age have found the career market competitive. Persons are competing against others having similar skills and credentials, and often having advanced degrees.

Tips for Self-Assessment

- Why should I organize my search for employment leads?
- How should I go about organizing my career search?
- What are the advantages of conducting an organized search?

You can easily feel frustrated or depressed while searching for the perfect career setting. These feelings often result when you have been turned down for a career opening, when your application is not accepted, or when few openings are available in your field. Other factors which may bring on negative feelings are your personal fears, perceived barriers, missed opportunities, unfulfilled expectations, or lack of interest. You can avoid negative feelings by developing an organized plan to meet your objectives. Many persons experiencing frustration, embarrassment, and even bad luck have been unsuccessful in their career search simply because they failed to employ a systematic campaign. You can create your own success, or so-called luck, through planning. Not all career seekers who get hired are the most qualified or have the best skills. Persons who are knowledgable of how to attain a career position are often the ones who have success in being employed.

The purpose of this chapter is to discuss the methods and resources which will help you secure information about possible career opportunities. The information and suggested steps may help reduce your frustration as you seek employment leads.

ORGANIZING YOUR RESEARCH

Tips for Self-Assessment

- What are my career goals?
- How can I organize my plan of action around these career goals?

SET GOALS FOR YOURSELF

You might begin with a plan of action; that is, develop a plan which will help you attain your career goal(s). First, search for a career opportunity rather than a job. Seek a particular career suited to your talents, abilities, and interests. Second, choose a career which offers opportunities for future development and advancement. Look for an opportunity—an opening where you can show that you are capable of outstanding service. Focus most of your time and effort on these career opportunities.

Your plan should include short-term objectives to help you meet your overall career goals. You may also benefit from establishing a time schedule which lists each objective and when you complete each.

In short, identify the particular kind of career which you desire. Then identify those potential career settings where you can obtain this type of career.

DeVry Institute

ON - CAMPUS RECRUITING
SUMMER - FALL TERM

CAREER COUNSELING
AND
PLACEMENT

Plan your career search as an organized campaign from the outset.

USE YOUR TIME WISELY

You will need to spend a fair amount of time in your career search. Each day should include a period spent on career research. The primary activities in your search will be self-analysis, planning, reading printed materials, informational interviewing, making phone calls, and visiting the library and friends.

CONSIDER YOUR PREFERRED GEOGRAPHICAL LOCATION

In what region of the United States or in what other country might you choose to perform your career? You should seriously consider where you would prefer working before beginning your research. You may want to locate in a particular section of the country rather than make yourself available for any opportunity. The more specific your preference, the more limited your opportunities may be; however, in many careers, by selecting certain locations, you may limit your opportunities in number but actually increase your chances of being offered a position. For instance, many small communities throughout the Unitied States are searching for family doctors. Few medical doctors choose these locations. While limited opportunities exist in these communities, doctors who want to practice in those locations are practically assured of obtaining their career choice. Considering where you want to be employed can help you decide which career leads to collect and which to eliminate.

EXPLORING RESOURCES FOR EMPLOYMENT

Tips for Self-Assessment

- How familiar am I with various sources of information about employment vacancies or opportunities?
- How can I evaluate these sources to obtain the best possible leads and avoid the less promising ones?

After having determined the limitations you intend to impose on career opportunities, you will be ready to conduct specific research. You can use a number of sources for this effort. The value of each source will vary according to the facilities in any section of the country and to the type of career you seek. Regardless of the relative value, explore each source in order to find the maximum number of opportunities.

Locating good career leads involves knowing how to locate as many potential employers as possible from various sources and attaining pertinent information to determine which ones will be better options than others. You will use your best leads to contact the most promising employers.

CAREER LEADS IN NEWSPAPERS

Newspapers—local, metropolitan, and national—have traditionally been the most common source for career leads. Yet, this most familiar method in career hunting is not necessarily the most productive. To focus your career research solely on help wanted ads would be unwise.

Most career opportunities rarely reach the help-wanted advertisement section of the newspaper. Thus, if you depend solely on the newspaper for career leads, you will limit your opportunities for employment. You will be missing about 75 percent of the other employers who could be interested in your skills and abilities. When a want ad advertises a position in the newspaper, the competition for that position will increase. Career leads advertised in large metropolitan newspapers frequently ellicit several hundred applicants. Read and respond to appropriate newspaper advertisements but do not spend your time solely on them.

SOURCES OF NEWSPAPER LEADS

You will find most career leads in newspapers of large urban areas in the classified pages each Sunday. Local newspapers may also contain leads. If you are considering relocating to another area, newspapers from other cities or neighboring areas will be important to your research. Many trade or professional journals, magazines, and newsletters in your career field often list leads. The *National Business Employment Weekly* is a good source of career leads in a variety of fields, although many ads suggest openings for middle- and upper-level careers. This periodical contains articles and suggestions to maximize your chances of obtaining a position. The *Wall Street Journal* also provides good leads for employment; however, career offerings in both the *Wall Street Journal* and *National Business Employment Weekly* may require you to relocate to geographical areas different from your own. Likewise, the Sunday editions of large metropolitan newspapers—the *New York Times,* the *Dallas Morning News,* or the *Los Angeles Times*—include a classified section, but many openings in these papers may also require you to relocate. (The Sunday classified ad section of the *New York Times* is not included outside its metropolitan area.) You might contact friends or relatives and ask them to send promising newspapers to you which are outside your area. You might also opt to write to your preferred newspaper for a Sunday subscription.

CAREER WANT ADS

Career want ads are generally one of four types—open ads, blind ads, smorgasbord ads, and glamour ads. Being aware of what these ads mean and how they differ can help you attain the best available leads.

Open ads include both a description of the position and the name of the employing organization. An open ad, such as the one in Figure 7–1, will be most helpful. By knowing the position and the organization, you will investigate only situations which appear to fit your career plans. Your competition is likely to be greater with open ads than blind ads.

ADVERTISING SALESMAN

Needed for Christian radio station KOCV in OKC. Energetic, aggressive professional with proven sales experience. Top pay based on results! Management growth potential. Send resume and references to:

Rich Bott, KOCV Radio
1919 N. Broadway
Oklahoma City, OK 73101

FIGURE 7–1

Blind ads do not indicate the name of the employer and often omit the type of business and career title. Replies to the ads are usually directed to a box number. Employers use blind ads to limit the number of applications they must send, to avoid the necessity of acknowledging phone calls or interviewing unqualified applicants, and to keep recruitment confidential. Some companies do not let their employees or other companies know of the vacancy.

A blind ad may advertise a position which does not exist. A company or even a personnel agency might be determining if there are qualified and available career seekers. Some companies place blind ads to determine which of their employees are seeking employment elsewhere. You will probably gain little, if anything, from blind ads. But, should you give up and not pursue blind ads? No, because most ads are this type. You should search cautiously and attempt to find ads for a position outside your present work setting. Then you should find out whether the company is considering hiring for any position, including your own. (You certainly would not want to apply for your own position.) To remain anonymous, use a post office box address rather than your mailing address. This approach is similar to the employer who uses a blind ad. You also might want to submit an unsigned cover letter and a resumé without your name and real address. Limit your use of facts about your background and indicate the importance of not revealing your identity until the company of the blind ad shows an interest in you. These strategies are useful in cases where you are unsure about a company submitting a blind ad. Keep in mind that 80 percent of career want ads are blind ads. See Figure 7–2.

The *smorgasbord ad* in Figure 7–3 lists many career positions in a variety of fields. These ads generally come from personnel agencies who purchase large advertising space from newspapers at reduced costs. Remember that agencies frequently place more want ads than they have positions available, in order to attract career seekers to register for employment. Although these ads are attractive, pass them up. You probably will not lose any opportunities.

FBO BASE MANAGER
Northeast U.S. base of growing national chain requires 3–5 years successful management experience in large department, knowledge of line services, airlines, and aircraft maintenance. Excellent opportunity for good pay, benefits, and future advancement. Send resume and salary requirement to:

Box EF-263
Wall Street Journal

FIGURE 7–2

ALL FEES PAID

CAREER SECYS

RECEPTIONIST

$10,800+   Fee PD

Plush organization needs out-going personality for busy front desk.
Horizon phone experience helps, but not mandatory.

RECPT/SECY

$12–$13,000   Fee PD

Prestigious attorneys need receptionist for variety position. Some typing
required. Benefits and great advancement opportunity.

SECT/RECPT

$10,200   Fee PD

Real estate executives need front desk receptionist for variety career.
Heavy contact with the public. Good typing skills required.

BANK SECY

$9,900+   Fee PD

Chance for advancement! Super career opportunity. Free medical.

CUSTOMER SERVICE

$11,000   Fee PD

Need someone with a variety of clerical skills for clerical service. Start
your career now!

521-9953
TOMORROW UNLIMITED
4001 N. Classen, Suite 100
Chestnut City, Utah 74589

FIGURE 7–3

Charm or appeal ads, which directly or indirectly state that you can
earn large sums of money without too much work, are gimmicks to attract
your attention. You can easily identify this advertising by its wording and its
unclear description of the duties and skills (if they are stated) needed to
perform the job. See Figure 7–4. These ads appeal to your personality.
Again, ignore this type of want ad. You have more to gain by looking at
more promising sources.

Situation wanted ads, see Figure 7–5, are personal advertisements
which you, the career seeker, place in the newspaper to attract potential
employers. Employers read situation wanted ads when they seek an individual with a particular set of qualifications. If you place this type of
advertisement, you should be ready to accept a position immediately.
Usually, persons who place situation wanted ads are consultants, who have

---

MEN & WOMEN

If you are tired of sitting at home, ride with Dan Julian and see how you can make $100 a day or better. Must have your own transportation. For further information call 942-8511 Monday thru Thursday 7 p.m.–10 p.m. and ask for Dan Julian.

FIGURE 7–4

special services to provide a business for a limited period of time, or persons who have special skills or career qualifications.

You must pay a fee to the newspaper to publish your ad. The size and length of the ad will determine its cost. Can you afford a situation wanted ad, or should you concentrate your career research on tangible leads? If you decide to run an ad, which newspapers, magazines, journals, or newsletters will have the greatest number of readers in your career field? How can you write your ad to attract potential employers? You must be the one to answer all these questions.

JOURNALS AND NEWSLETTERS

Most professional fields are affiliated with some type of organization which produces regular issues of a journal or newsletter for its members. The issues contain articles which help members stay abreast of changes in their career field. Many journals also contain employment advertisements. Issues of the *Management Accountant,* published by Mailbu Publishing Company, and issues of the *Accounting Review,* published by the American Accounting Association, present professional articles, sales ads, and classified ads of career leads for their members.

Journals and newsletters often provide information about professional activities such as meetings, conventions, conferences, and workshops. By

---

Xerox operator 9400 9500, day shift or weekends. 521-3626 between 8 & 5. After 5, 733-0588.

Need 5 nights a week, licensed boiler operator, 14 yrs exp. Also do floors. After 4:30, 437-8237.

FIGURE 7–5

attending these activities, you can meet other professionals who might provide you with potential employers. At many of these meetings, company and business representatives will be seeking out and interviewing potential employees. The leads you attain at these activities may positively change your career future.

How can you learn of professional activities? Go to your school or public library and look for the following reference books: *Scientific and Technical Societies in the United States and Canada*, the *Directory of National Trade and Professional Associations in the United States, Career Guide to Professional Associations*, and the *Encyclopedia of Associations*. In each of these references you will find names and addresses of various professional groups. Contact the professional groups which interest you and inquire about their journal or newsletter.

You can also find names of professional journals by looking in resources which list articles pertaining to specialized career fields. Resource books which will help you identify names of journals are *Oceanic Index, Education Index, Dentistry Index, Applied Science and Technology Index, Humanities Index, Engineering Index, Biological and Agricultural Index, Hospital Literature Index, Industrial Arts Index, Social Science Index, Business Periodicals Index, Environment Index, Accountant's Index, Music Index,* and *Art Index*. In other sources, including the *Readers Guide to Periodical Literature*, you may find references to current articles about your career interest(s) bearing names of professional journals. Once you have identified names of journals or periodicals, you can often find their addresses by looking in the front or back of the reference index or by looking for their names in the *Working Press* or *Ayer's Dictionary*.

If you are considering relocating to another geographical area, you might invest some time in reading the local paper of that particular place. You can find the addresses of various newspapers and their subscription rates in the *Ayer Dictionary of Publications*, which contains information on numerous magazines and newspapers in the United States and Canada. Another source is volume one of *The Working Press of the Nation*, which contains the names of daily, weekly, and special interest newspapers in the United States and Canada.

Trade journals provide helpful information about industrial groups, for example, accounting, data processing, finance, insurance, and real estate. Trade journal publications provide information about specific industrial groups' achievements and concerns. Since these publications usually do not advertise career openings, you may need to contact preferred individual businesses for industrial or trade information. Volume two of the *Working Press of the Nation* will help you become familiar with various trade journals as well as show you where to contact businesses within your preferred trade or industry.

READING NEWSPAPER OR MAGAZINE LEADS

As you look for career leads in newspapers and magazines, read the classified want ad section in an orderly manner; that is, go through the entire section. Notice that career leads which interest you will not necessarily appear under systematic headings. Generally, editors list newspaper career leads by career title and arrange them in alphabetical order. Should a business advertise for an assistant editor, a newspaper would likely list it under the letter *A*. Knowing newspapers use alphabetical listings might be an advantage for you. Many career seekers qualified for an assistant editor position would probably look at the listings under the letter *E* for editor.

Sometimes, you find advertisements which give incorrect or vague career descriptions. For example, the career title may not match the description and/or duties listed. You may even find a description of one career which sounds more like another. The career title may be so unclear that you have difficulty determining what the position involves. For instance, the career title, group researcher manager, might require interpersonnel, investigative, or leadership duties. Clearly, you should not concentrate on career titles.

A career may be listed in the wrong category. You might find an editing position for a sports manufacturer under *sports*. A business or technical category might include opportunities for writers or public relations workers. Read more than one section of the want ads, so you will be able to locate all the worthwhile leads. Place each on a sheet of paper, and record the name of the newspaper or magazine and the ad's publication date. You can use each sheet as a career contact log, with an employment ad attached to it. Enter the date that you answered the ad.

Systematically use a portion of each day responding to ads which seem promising. When a potential employer responds to you, enter the date on the sheet. Also, state whether the response was a personal or form letter. Using this approach, you are likely to stay on top of your reading and responding to employment leads.

TELEVISION AND RADIO LEADS

Many television and radio broadcasts include employment leads. In metropolitan areas, such as Chicago, Illinois, and Tulsa, Oklahoma, television and radio stations schedule particular times during the day, such as early mornings, for announcements of employment openings to the general public. These announcements usually include openings only in the local areas. Some educational television stations broadcast career leads too. Many television and radio programs include strategies for obtaining employment, such as interview techniques. You can expect the competition for television and radio leads to be high, since many other career hunters will be aware of and responding to them.

To find the broadcast times of employment announcement programs in your area, check the television and radio sections of your newspaper. You might also write or phone the local television and radio stations.

GOVERNMENT EMPLOYMENT AGENCIES

In general, there are two types of employment agencies—*non-governmental*, which are private and charge fees, and *governmental*, which are public and provide no-cost assistance. Government employment agencies can be a source of career opportunities.

The United States federal government can steer you towards a wide variety of career fields within its complex organizational system. The Office of Personnel Management offers information about career opportunities within the federal government. Ten regional offices are located throughout the United States: Atlanta, Georgia; Chicago, Illinois; Denver, Colorado; Dallas, Texas; Seattle, Washington; Boston, Massachusetts; Philadelphia, Pennsylvania; New York, New York; San Francisco, California; and St. Louis, Missouri. The central office of the Office of Personnel Management is located in Washington, DC. You can secure career literature and inquire about career opportunities with the federal government either by writing or telephoning (toll-free number listed under United States Government) your regional office.

You may want to consider an upper-level, professional career with the federal government. If you have an undergraduate degree or comparable experience in management, professional, or technical areas, you may qualify for a government service position by taking PACE, the Professional and Administrative Career Examination. Study guides are available to help you become familiar with the PACE, for example, *Barron's How to Prepare for the Professional and Administrative Career Examination,* written by Delores H. Bright. You can borrow this study material from a library or purchase it at a bookstore. The testing schedule for this examination, as well as other information, is available through your regional Office of Personnel Management.

State, county, and city employment agencies provide employment leads and career counseling services in addition to administering unemployment insurance and worker's compensation. Many career hunters find their experiences with this kind of agency to be depressing since most employment leads are for low-level careers. In metropolitan areas, you can expect your competition to be high for most of these leads because the city agency has given many persons the same lead to explore. Should you consider your state employment agency? Yes, but you should also consider other sources for employment leads as well. Remember, one lead might be better than no lead at all.

County and city governments' personnel offices are other sources which provide career leads. These offices usually have lists and announcements about specific career openings for county and city government employment. You might phone, write, or make a personal visit to these offices for leads in your area of interest.

PROFESSIONAL ASSOCIATIONS AND ORGANIZATIONS

Many professional associations and organizations provide placement services to their members, who might be searching for career opportunities. Usually, these groups have contact with potential employers and announce employment opportunities in their journals and newsletters. Persons searching for positions often publish their situation wanted ads in associations' or organizations' journals where potential employers may read them.

Many organizations mail descriptions of career opportunities to their entire membership or post career opportunities on bulletin boards at conferences, meetings, and conventions. If you are interested in finding employment in a chosen field, contact associations for specific information, such as conference meeting schedules, career placement services, and registration procedures.

PERSONNEL AGENCIES AND EXECUTIVE RECRUITMENT FIRMS

Tips for Self-Assessment

- How can employment agencies help me obtain career opportunities?
- What are the advantages and disadvantages of using a private employment agency?

Personnel agencies and recruitment firms often assist career seekers. Their basic purpose is to secure employment openings from businesses and search for potential candidates to send on interviews. Both personnel agencies and recruitment firms usually charge fees. They may charge you for their service, or they may charge the employer who is looking for someone to fill a position. In some cases an employer seeking to fill a high-level or specialized position will pay an agency or recruitment firm a fee after he has chosen a candidate. If this is not the case, you, the applicant, may be charged a fixed fee or a percentage of your salary once you have accepted a position.

Many executive search firms specialize in placing high-level business people. These firms often have career leads for positions in the range of $25,000 per year (and up). Personnel agencies usually offer positions at lower salary ranges. Many personnel agencies specialize in career fields; whereas, usually search firms do not.

Search firms normally work with business executives who request their services. Usually, these firms do not accept resumés unless they have requested them; however, you may acquire names and addresses of search firms by contacting top executives in various businesses. You also might write and request a list of names and addresses of search firms from the American Management Association, 135 West 50th Street, New York, NY 10019.

CHOOSING A PERSONNEL AGENCY

Since some personnel agencies are better than others, what should you keep in mind as you choose an agency? Better agencies are likely to have placed persons in a variety of career fields. Usually, this kind of agency works in a business-like fashion and will not push you to make on-the-spot decisions.

Many states require personnel agencies and search firms to be licensed before offering their services to both career seekers and employers; however, this is not the case for individual staff workers within each agency. Because an individual worker may not have the necessary credentials to certify his capabilities as a placement counselor, you might be more qualified in that position than he is.

As stated earlier, many personnel agencies specialize in placing career seekers in a specific field. Such an agency in your career field can provide leads which may interest you; whereas, other agencies will provide leads from various fields. You might be able to identify the career focus of an agency by studying many of the agency's ads and determining which fields are most advertised. You can also ask friends and persons in business to identify reputable agencies and search firms for you. Some professional organizations and counseling services may suggest reputable agencies and firms. You can request a copy of the *Employment Agency Directory,* a listing of agencies who are members of the National Employment Association, by writing to the Employment Agency Directory, National Employment Association, 200 K Street, N.W., Washington, DC 20006.

In many cases, fees are paid by the employer; however, an agency may hold you responsible for fees not covered by an employer. It is not uncommon for a business to contact not only an employment agency but to advertise in newspapers, magazines, newsletters. Read the conditions of the contract which an employer may ask you to sign. Your signature, depending on the conditions, could legally require you to pay all fees, although you found the lead through another source.

Finally, an agency may require you to sign forms before it can check out the references which you have listed on your application. Your refusal to sign this statement will delay your career search and placement. By federal law, an agency is not allowed to contact references, if you have not given permission in writing. Adherence to this law may be particularly crucial if you are still employed, searching for a position elsewhere, and do not want your present employer made aware of the search. You might consider signing the form but include the condition that the agency not contact your present employer.

COLLEGE OR UNIVERSITY
CAREER PLACEMENT SERVICES

Most colleges and universities offer placement services to their graduates. As a graduate, you might contact your college placement office or alumni association to determine your eligibility for its placement service. College placement services receive and distribute employment leads biweekly or monthly to their registered graduates. Other services may include on-campus interviews with business representatives (or recruiters), interview techniques, resumé assistance, and referenced materials of career placement publications. One publication which can be of help is the *College Placement Annual*, containing career requirements and the addresses of more than a thousand employers in government and industry. You can find this book in the college placement office or the library.

UNCOVERING THE HIDDEN MARKETPLACE

Tips for Self-Assessment

- What are the best ways for me to uncover employment leads which exist within internal organizations?
- How can I establish a system to obtain leads continually?

Most persons seeking employment are familiar with sources obtained through newspapers, journals, television and radio, and personnel agencies. Few career hunters recognize potential employment opportunities in the hidden marketplace. The hidden career marketplace is located in organizational or industrial settings where employees work. This hidden marketplace, an internal career placement system within a business, offers career opportunities to its employees. Often an employer seeks potential employees from outside a company, as well as inside, long before announcing the opening to the general public. In some cases, the general public rarely hears of a vacant position. Few, if any, of these opportunities become known to persons outside the internal organization or industry; therefore, these employment leads remain hidden to most of us.

How can someone learn of these employment opportunities within an industry? Just as we are continually changing, so do companies and their needs. Companies frequently must hire additional workers for various positions. Individuals retiring, in most instances, will require placements within the organization. As businesses expand through establishing additional branch offices in new locations, enlarging a department, or merging with another company, new positions may come into existence. Some companies are awarded federal monies to conduct projects which require additional workers. Available positions occur when a business must replace persons who were fired; persons who permanently leave the company; persons who make vertical, lateral, or backward career moves; or persons who are on extended sick leave.

As positions become available, a business's internal career placement staff will often announce openings through the company's newsletter or newspaper. The personnel department will also visibly post career announcements inside the work setting.

By federal law, employers are prohibited from not making employment vacancies known to the general public. As part of this law, an affirmative action plan encourages employers to publicly announce employment vacancies. In spite of this plan, you are still unsure of which employers operate using affirmative action and which do not. Many employers, who believe their company is not dependent upon the federal government for monies or contracts, do not feel obligated to follow any hiring practice except their own.

PENETRATING THE HIDDEN MARKETPLACE

You are not likely to read announcements of new career openings in a particular company, but you might get some ideas about what will become available by personally contacting the company. This contact requires that you first determine what a company needs and define the services you can provide to meet those needs. You need to determine which person in a high position with hiring capacity to contact. For example, a company having problems with falling sales could use someone's special skills in marketing and advertising. Such a company might require you to provide a written plan describing how you would improve sales. You should strive to find employers having forthcoming needs, which are not yet widely advertised. To locate such employers means that you must conduct an aggressive campaign to market yourself.

You may also penetrate the hidden marketplace by writing a letter to the right person within a particular company. A powerful letter to the person who makes the hiring decisions, detailing how your services and expertise can benefit the company, could certainly generate potential employment for you. You could be just the person a company is considering to head up their new downtown insurance branch! This approach may sound like a long shot to you, but what do you have to lose other than postage for the letter? More importantly, do not limit the power of your letter.

NURTURING YOUR CAREER CONTACTS

Nurturing personal contacts may be one valuable way to increase career leads. In many instances, personal contacts yield employment opportunities when all else seems unproductive. Although you may be unaware of them, you already have personal contacts who can help you, such as friends, family members, former employers, associates, former teachers or professors, trade association executives, and colleagues. Which one of these groups actually knows that you are on a career campaign? Imagine how many leads—businesses with employment openings, names and addresses of persons with power to hire you, or other suggestions—you could have if others knew about your employment situation. To increase your leads, you must increase your contacts and inform them that you are searching for career opportunities. Let others know of your career interests, and ask them questions. Develop a systematic program to locate potential career leads.

PYRAMIDING YOUR CONTACT LEADS

Try to increase, or pyramid, your leads from each person, so that you are continually adding to the information you already have obtained.

Meeting persons at professional conferences and conventions can provide a wealth of career information. Use this opportunity to become acquainted with new persons and gain new leads which will direct you toward specific career opportunities. Company representatives, as well as professionals from various parts of the United States, often attend meetings, seminars, conferences, conventions, trade fairs, and special workshops. The number of persons attending some of these activities can range into the

Conferences and conventions provide a wealth of career information—including leads to positions that might fall open.

thousands. Information you gain from persons at just one professional activity may well lead you closer to your career goal(s). Try to build one employment lead upon another, along with other important information. This process will maximize your career options.

CREATING NETWORK CONTACTS

Developing individual contacts is an informal way to build networks of associations. Formal (and informal) groups and organizations meet throughout this country to provide career seekers support, guidance, resource materials, and leads. Such networks can help many persons, including women, ethnic minority group members, physically handicapped, displaced homemakers, middle-aged furlowed workers, or furlowed executives who are searching for employment opportunities. Some of these groups' meetings may be held in public places within your local area.

To obtain information from these groups or organizations you must

1. Make the first contact. Describe your situation to a member of the group and talk about your career interests and skills.
2. Ask the member for help. Determine if the person is aware of leads which meet your skills and career interests. Do not give up if she does not respond to your question—try again until you are reasonably satisfied that you have been answered.
3. Log all information for a later reference. Record your leads and list the names of those who supplied the leads so you can check out the information. Using the name of the person who gave you the lead might at least get you an interview.
4. Request your contact person to stay in touch. Ask your contact to call you if he has information. Remember to leave your name, address, and phone number, so your contact can reach you about a lead or so he can pass your resumé to the right source.
5. Keep your network productive. For instance, if your contact is unable to provide the kinds of information you need, ask the person if she would provide names and addresses of other persons who might be able to assist you.
6. Follow up your contacts at various times to obtain new leads and let them know that you are still in need of their assistance.

DETERMINING WHETHER
I QUALIFY FOR A LEAD

Now that you have gathered your employment leads, consider whether you and each of the leads make a *good fit*. Obviously, your skills will not match the requirements of all leads. You will need to determine whether your skills, interests, lifestyle, or desires are similar to each employment opportunity.

Tips for Self-Assessment

- Now that I have found some leads, which of these make good sense for me?
- What do I know about the organization behind each of my leads?
- How can I find information about various organizations?

You should also be aware of what each employer wants as he looks for someone to fill the position. Does it make much sense to invest energy searching out a lead when you know that you do not meet the required skills? No, you probably should not spend time pursuing this type of lead. Do the requirements of the position suggest that your personal needs will be met? A lead may offer a big salary and an opportunity to travel across the country, but traveling and being away from your family may not satisfy your lifestyle or values. Career satisfaction requires that both you and the company are satisfied with each other.

Having a strong urge to attain a position, some of us lose sight of what we can bring to a potential employer and what the employer can provide for us. Often, we do not allow sufficient time to check out an employment lead—the company and the position. To determine which leads are best suited for you, collect more information about a position and the company than what is generally advertised. For instance, try to learn as much information now about a potential employer and a specific position as you would normally find out in, say, two to six months. Information in journals, newsletters, and newspapers or passed to you through individuals and network contacts is not always complete or clear. The following ads in Figures 7–6 and 7–7, for example, tell little or, in one case, nothing about the responsibilities of the position.

ASSISTANT CONTROLLER

The Los Gatos Corporate Headquarters of an International Construction Firm, specializing in pre-stressed concrete, rock stabilization and transportation systems seeks a Professional Accountant for a staff position. Responsibilities include assisting the Corporate Controller in reporting to management and performing special administrative projects. CPA Certificate and experience in related industry required. For immediate consideration, please send your resume and salary requirements to: Corporate Controller, VSL Corporation, 101 Albright Way, Los Gatos, California 95030.

FIGURE 7–6

FINANCIAL PRODUCT PLANNER

Leading edge financial services company seeks state of the art innovator of credit instruments. Strong analytical qualitative skills needed. Must know underlying mechanics of traditional credit instruments and be able to apply creative new credit concepts to both existing and untapped markets.

Three years experience in financial and credit analysis with a recognized financial service organization, plus M.B.A. required. Send resume including current earnings in complete confidence to:

The Management Group
274 Madison Avenue, Suite 1500A
New York, New York 10016

FIGURE 7-7

Having a detailed description of the position in Figure 7–7, outlining its duties, responsibilities, salary, and fringe benefits would help you, the career seeker. The ad does not state the closing date for acceptance of applications, and you probably know little or nothing about the company. Will you have enough time to collect sufficient information to fill in the blanks of unanswered questions? It makes little sense gathering information about an employment lead if you are unable to obtain that information before the closing date or submitting your application. Your initial move should be to phone or write the company to determine the closing date to apply. Realizing duties and responsibilities may vary from one company to the next, you could contact another company, having a similar position to the one in the ad, and ask them for a job description of their position. Completing this last suggestion can also help you arrive at your decision of whether to follow a lead. Having sufficient information and time are essential in making a good evaluation.

Now you have some avenues for learning about the positions listed in advertisements or given by *word of mouth*. You *must* obtain information about the company or employer before making your decision.

BECOMING KNOWLEDGEABLE OF PROSPECTIVE EMPLOYERS

If time permits, thoroughly investigate your prospective employer. You should learn about a prospective company, a top company executive, or both, in order to make your decision about following your employment lead.

Find out what the prospective company manufactures and what services it provides. Be aware of what is new at this company and in the industry. Municipal Hospital, along with most of the health care industry, has recently installed medical computers to aid in diagnosing and servicing its patients.

You can use standard reference sources at your local or college library to obtain information about various companies. These references can help you in a number of ways. For example, Kim, an accounting student who will graduate next month, recently received an offer from a small company to begin work at almost double the accountant's average salary. She decided to investigate the financial standing of the company. After discovering the company had a poor rating, she decided not to accept the company's offer. Kim's investigation benefited her because this company filed bankruptcy six months later. Similarly, a medical technologist can find out about a hospital's medical facilities, a news editor can determine the circulation of a leading business magazine, or an engineer can learn what types of federal government contracts an engineering firm has been awarded.

You might use the following references about various companies:

Moody's Manuals   These texts provide financial and background information, describe services offered, name principal officers, and cite geographical locations. Types of businesses profiled are municipals and governments, railroads, public utilities, industries, banks, insurance companies, and other financial agencies.

Poor's Register of Directors and Executives   This register lists numerous corporations, including address, products, and number of employees. It alphabetically lists directors and executives, gives brief biographical data, and names other companies where these persons are directors. An obituary and new-names section appears.

Thomas' Register of American Manufacturers   The five volumes of this register include information on company names, addresses, and telephone numbers, branch offices, products, capital ratings, and company officials.

Dunn and Bradstreet   This reference geographically organizes business firms and evaluates their financial responsibility and type of business.

Encyclopedia Business Information Source   This text lists primary subjects of interest to managerial personnel and also includes a record of sourcebooks, periodicals, organizations, directories, handbooks, and bibliographies on each topic.

Chamber of Commerce Directories   These directories generally contain the major local industries including their addresses, products, and number of employees. Most cities, some states, and many metropolitan areas publish such directories.

To obtain information on individuals who are employed at the companies which you are considering, particularly those individuals who make hiring decisions, use the following reference sources located in your public or college library.

International Businessmen's Who's Who This text is concerned with international trade and includes biographical sketches of prominent figures engaged in export, import, and related fields from sixty of the world's largest countries.

Who's Who in Finance and Industry This source profiles international businessmen. An index of firms, with references to personnel, is presented.

Dunn and Bradstreet Reference Book of Corporate Managements This reference provides brief biographical information about officers and directors of close to 2,400 companies. Companies appear in alphabetical order along with an index of principal officers.

Who's Who in America Best known and generally the most useful of the current biographical works, this text includes information about persons of national prominence.

Who's Who in the West; Who's Who in the Midwest; Who's Who in the East; Who's Who in the South and Southwest; Who's Who in New York; Who's Who in Oklahoma; American Men and Women of Science; and Directory of American Scholars All contain useful biographical information about persons of state, regional, scientific, and educational prominence.

In conclusion, career planning requires that you systematically organize the steps of your career search. These steps include marketing yourself. While trying to discover a career opportunity, you will have to do a bit of salespersonship—you are selling your services. To market your services, investigate opportunities and determine which businesses could use your services, where they are located, and what features or skills will especially appeal to prospective employers. Analyze your skills in relationship to the requirements of available employment leads. Finally, you must bring your skills or services to the attention of the most promising prospective employers through resumés and interviews.

POINTS TO REVIEW

1. As you organize your career research, set goals for yourself, use your time wisely, and consider your preferred geographical location.
2. To locate good employment leads, you should gather as many prospective employers as possible from a variety of sources and gather sufficient

information about each to determine which ones are better options than others.

3. Although newspapers are traditionally the most common source for career leads, they are not necessarily the most beneficial or productive means for securing employment. Only 25 percent of employment leads are advertised in newspapers.

4. Focus your attention on newspaper ads, but do not spend your time and efforts solely on newspapers.

5. Some nationally distributed newspapers which you might use in your career research are the *Wall Street Journal*, the *National Business Employment Weekly*, the *New York Times*, the *Dallas Morning News*, and the *Los Angeles Times*.

6. Five types of employment want ads are open ads, blind ads, smorgasbord ads, charm or appeal ads, and situation wanted ads.

7. Ads in newspapers and magazines may be classified in an unsystematic order and will require your going through the entire section.

8. Professional journals and newsletters often provide helpful information about meetings, conventions, conferences, and workshops. These activities will enable you to meet professional members who could provide you with several potential employers.

9. Many television and radio stations provide employment leads.

10. You can obtain career opportunities through the U.S. federal government and state, county, and city employment agencies.

11. Professional associations, personnel agencies, and executive recruitment firms are sources of potential employment leads.

12. Federal laws prohibit many employers from not making career vacancies known to the general public.

13. By developing your personal contacts, pyramiding, and networking you can penetrate the hidden marketplace.

14. Steps to obtain information from networks are (a) making contact with persons who want to help, (b) requesting their help, (c) recording your information for future reference, (d) asking your contacts to keep in touch, (e) keeping your networks productive, and (f) following up your contacts and, at different times, informing them of your need for new leads.

15. A relatively *good fit* between what you can offer a prospective employer and what the employer can provide for you should exist before you contact your leads of potential employers.

16. To determine whether you and potential employers make a *good fit,* you gather detailed information about both the position you are considering and the employer or company who is offering the position.

Experiential Exercises

1. List some *advantages* and *disadvantages* of the five types of employment ads.

   Open Ads

   Blind Ads

   Smorgasbord Ads

   Charm or Appeal Ads

   Situation Wanted Ads

2. A well-written employment ad includes important information about a career lead. As you read an employment ad, determine if all the information you need appears. Read the following employment ad.

SENIOR PACKAGING ENGINEER

At Brown's Cosmetics, quality is a way of life. And it shows . . . in our products, our technology, and our people. We are currently seeking a Senior Packaging Engineer, with a proven record of on-time project completions, to join our carefully selected team of professionals in Dallas.

This position requires a Bachelor's degree in Package Engineering or a related field, and a minimum of 5 years experience in specification and evaluation of finished packages and components. In-depth knowledge of plastic bottles, closures, and injection molded parts preferred. Experience in a consumer goods industry with automated, high-speed packaging equipment is mandatory.

In return for outstanding commitment and performance, you will have an exceptional opportunity for recognition and compensation relative to your contributions.

For immediate consideration, send your resumé, with salary history to:

Attn: Personnel Manager
Brown's Cosmetics, Inc.
1330 Regal Row
Tuscon, AZ 75247

Resumé must contain salary history to be considered.

Using the following list, indicate which information the employment ad provides.

a. Career title

b. Duties and responsibilities

c. Other requirements (relocation, travel, or provide own tools)

d. Educational requirements (or preferred education)

   e. Required experience and skills (or preferred skills)

   f. Salary

   g. Benefits (including paid insurance and vacation)

   h. Opportunities for career advancement

   i. Ways to respond to the ad

3. Assume that you might be interested in the previous advertisement. You will need some important additional information before making a commitment to contact the employer. Based on your examination of the ad, list the steps which you would use to obtain this missing information.

4. How could you locate names of professional journals in your specialized career field?

5. List steps you would take while reading through newspaper and magazine employment ads.

6. Developing a sound network of contact persons, who will share employment leads, depends on your ability to contact as many persons as possible. Which members of your family (including cousins, aunts, and uncles) can you list who might be good contacts for employment leads?

7. Which members of your community (for example, neighbors, chamber of commerce officials, and former teachers and employers) can you list as contacts who might provide information about employment opportunities?

8. List key officials (or members) of professional organizations who you can contact about employment opportunities.

Person's Name   *Organization*

9. List professional organizations related to your field of interest which hold conferences, conventions, workshops, or meetings you might wish to attend in order to build career contacts.

10. The following is a career contact log which you can use as you list and follow up your contact leads. For purposes of this exercise, assume that you have a specific career interest. Fill in the appropriate spaces of the log with individuals who you think would provide leads for employment opportunities pertaining to your career interest.

Date	Individual Contacted	Position	Business and Location	Phone Number	Results of Lead	Thank-you Letter Forwarded

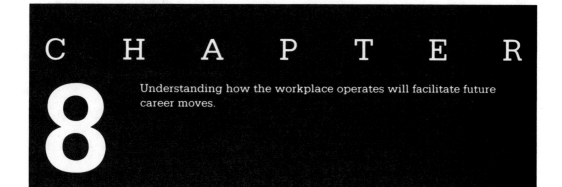

C H A P T E R

8

Understanding how the workplace operates will facilitate future career moves.

Getting Started and Moving Ahead in Your Career

As you plan your career, you resolve to make a good start and then, possibly, move up the career ladder. Your first days on the job can make a lasting impression on your employer. Your ability to become aware of the new working situation and to act accordingly will determine your beginning, including the relationship between you and your employer.

Tips for Self-Assessment

- How do I get off to a good start in my new career?
- How important will the way that I begin my new career affect my future?

How well do you fit into this new work environment? It is unlikely that you will be successful, if you and the company do not match. As a newcomer, you probably will be unable to make any major changes. You might be acting unwisely by making suggestions at this stage, unless asked.

177

It is not uncommon for seasoned workers at your workplace to be cautious of you, the newcomer, particularly if you have many ideas and express them freely. Consider earning the respect and confidence of persons within the workplace, not forcing your ideas on them. Talking less but listening more may smooth your first days on the job. Many of your co-workers may not accept changes or ideas from you, since they do not know why you made the suggestions. Some persons will recognize sound suggestions but not accept them coming from a less experienced and/or younger worker. Again, you must win your niche by wisely following the accepted behavior of the workplace. A fine beginning in your new career is important for success and future advancement.

MAKING A GOOD START

To succeed at your career is your goal. Your reputation as a worker will rest on how you perform in your present position. If you perform reasonably well, you may establish a foothold in your career field. Your initial position, the first rung on your career ladder, may lead to interesting work, an acceptable salary, and a chance to contribute to society. Even if your new position is only part-time or temporary, you should do your best.

Your new employer probably believes that you possess the necessary skills and services for your position, or he would not have hired you. Usually, one of the employer's aims is to assist you in your work, because replacing workers can be expensive. Still, you must assume the responsibility of doing your best. Consider the new position as a challenge, and determine that you will be successful in it. If you give yourself the satisfaction of knowing that you have more than met the demands of your career, you also will be improving your chances for future career success.

EXPECTATIONS OF A NEW POSITION

Tips for Self-Assessment

- To what extent should I expect to work toward the needs of the company (employer) in my new career?
- In what ways do I see myself benefiting from my career?

Perhaps you feel you must give your all in your new position but receive little from your employer. Generally, you can expect (a) professional training, (b) work experience, (c) credentials, (d) visible exposure, and (e) contacts.

Professional Training   Your new position will provide the required training for advancement in your career field. This training can be valuable.

Frequently, persons seek a position with certain businesses (Atlantic Telephone and Telegraph, Xerox, International Business Machines) because of the special training programs these companies provide their employees. Usually quite expensive, this training would otherwise be out of your financial range, if you cared to purchase it for yourself. Because training is often necessary, why not get it at the employer's expense?

Work Experience   The experience you gain while working in a new career will help you obtain future positions. Some jobs will give you a broad range of experiences; whereas, others may only provide a narrow range. The extent of your experience may influence your career choices or future moves. For example, you might choose a certain position over others because its job tasks include greater opportunities in your career field.

Credentials   Many career fields require that you possess professional credentials documenting who you say you are and what you have done. A new position may give you the chance to obtain your credentials. On-the-job training and/or experiences with a well-known employer will be valuable as you move to future opportunities. For instance, having professional credentials can make a difference in the starting salary in your next position. Many beginning employment seekers seriously consider whether to work for one company over another. For instance, one might have more valuable credentials having worked for Xerox than Bloomingdale Machines, since Xerox is better known throughout the United States and other countries. A new position will enable you to build professional credentials.

Exposure   Some positions afford you with frequent opportunities to meet other persons. A position as a company sales representative, who travels to various businesses, will certainly include more exposure than, say, a position as a desk clerk. Through your professional activities, you can be known to others. As your career goals change, having met many persons can increase your career options.

Professional Contacts   While you may have gotten exposure in your position, you may not have made meaningful contacts. These contacts know you and are in a position to help you advance. Working at a position where you make these contacts is to your benefit.

In short, some positions will offer most, or all, of these five factors, and others will not. You must ask yourself, how does my position measure up using these factors? If your answer is not very well, first remember that your present position offers far more than no position at all. In your job, you may need to take a little more time to develop desired contacts and exposure. In most positions you may only obtain experience after working for a period of time.

Ben Chandler

Your first day on the job will probably include an orientation to your tasks and responsibilities.

YOUR FIRST DAY AT WORK

Coming to work the first day is an interesting experience because many things will be new and different. You may like the challenge of facing this new situation. To be on time, arrive before the workday begins. Eventually, you will learn just how much time you must allow for heavy traffic, missed busses, subways, or other unknown delays. To be late on the first day will embarrass you as well as make a poor impression on your employer, in spite of the reason for your lateness.

Tips for Self-Assessment

- Since first impressions may be lasting ones, how can I make a positive impression on the others in my new work environment?
- Which of my strengths should I use the first day at work to improve my performance?
- What about me might I improve or change to make a better impression on others?

Usually, someone like the employer or supervisor will provide an orientation and explain your tasks and responsibilities. You might even go through a period of training prior to actually working. Or, the supervisor might give you a short explanation of your job tasks and start you to work right away. Listen carefully before starting. Ask questions in order to avoid later unnecessary interruptions. Your co-workers will probably assist in answering your questions or addressing your concerns. Focus on your work, but be friendly to your co-workers. They will be anxious to help, providing you have a good attitude. Your first day in the new position will be special.

CAREER HABITS TO LEARN AND USE

Tips for Self-Assessment

- How would I describe the strengths and weaknesses of my personal work qualities?
- How can I break old, unproductive qualities and assume responsible ones?

As you continue working, you will develop confidence in your ability to face the new job tasks. Remember that you must demonstrate personal qualities to attain success. Qualities such as dependability, efficiency, drive, honesty, consideration, respectfulness, orderliness, time management, and personal health are keys to success in all careers. Try to develop these personal qualities and practice them until they become part of your everyday behavior. They will not only help you succeed in your present position but will help you advance quickly up the career ladder to a responsible and satisfying position. Let us examine each of these qualities briefly.

Dependability   Your employer will expect you to follow certain rules and procedures. Initially, you might be unsure why some of the rules exist, but you will understand at a later time. Being absent or tardy for work when you feel like it may cost you your position, no matter how well you perform your work. As a dependable worker, plan to give a full day's work, get your work completed, and provide assistance to others when needed.

Efficiency   Completing your work smoothly and effectively suggests that you are capable. Your employer probably wants your work done correctly, quickly, and without delay. One of the best ways for you to demonstrate your value to the company is by completing tasks in reasonably short amounts of time. Your employer will consider the time you spend and your accuracy in evaluating your performance. Focus your efforts on required tasks during working hours. Your diligence will cause others to recognize you as an efficient worker. During work avoid dealing with personal matters, such as making personal phone calls, writing personal letters, or attending to personal grooming. They all detract from your career performance.

Drive   As soon as you are familiar with your position, develop the drive or get-up-and-go to move ahead with assigned tasks. Be sure that you understand your supervisor's instructions before beginning. Ask questions if you are unsure about the task or its instructions. Your supervisor will more gladly clarify an assignment than receive an incorrectly completed job. Remember, asking questions too frequently may eventually annoy the supervisor.

Honesty   Truthfulness and sincerity are important to your success at work. If the company can depend on you, they will value your services. It is not uncommon for workers to make mistakes occasionally, but the key here is admitting them openly and accepting suggestions to improve work performance. A business will value you as a dependable employee if it can rely on you to satisfactorily complete work for which you are responsible.

Consideration   Much of your success will depend on how well you get along with your supervisors and other co-workers. Your ability to control your expression of dislikes and/or anger and to work cooperatively with others will enable you to go a long way in attaining your career goals.

Respectfulness   Treat your co-workers courteously and warmly. Consider others' feelings when you realize that they may be in bad mood. Avoid nagging other workers and playing practical jokes on them. Bill, who works with you, is generally irritable during the mornings. Ms. Smith, your supervisor, is quite forgetful and usually talks too much. Maybe Jim, your co-worker, seems unsure of himself because he has a hard time making up his mind. Though it may not be easy, deal with these situations by remaining calm and not taking them too seriously. Remember, you want to be regarded as a respected, mature person.

Orderliness   Develop orderly habits of obtaining and caring for materials, tools, or equipment. Avoid needless waste or damage. Orderliness can enhance your work performance; disorder can detract from your work. For example, Marie has a good record for speed in typing, but she usually has difficulty locating letters, carbons, and other materials on her cluttered desk. Anthony has good possibilities of becoming an electronic engineer, but he often avoids cleaning and repairing his equipment. Anthony usually has problems locating materials or tools when he needs them momentarily.

Time Management   To obtain what you want from your career, consider how you manage your time. If you feel rushed, unsure of which direction to move, or usually have several things you need to do, you may not be managing time wisely. In your new position, you may find yourself faced with demands on your time which you have not had before. To work harder or longer may not help your situation. You do not want to become less sensitive to your own needs and demand too much of your time and effort.

Your work will be easier if you consider your physical and mental needs as you use your time. Each of us has a larger supply of energy at certain periods of the working day than others. You should plan to tackle your more demanding tasks during the first few hours of your day or whenever you have a high level of energy. You might reserve your less demanding tasks for your low energy periods, perhaps in the late morning or late afternoon.

Avoid over scheduling yourself, so that you will be able to deal with one task at a time. Proper scheduling will help you to avoid making mistakes which require additional time to correct. Time management will help you work in an orderly fashion as well as achieve many tasks.

Personal Health   How you perform your work tasks relates to your physical condition. Being tired while working limits your performance. Looking ill around your co-workers can make them feel uncomfortable. Therefore, keep your body healthy with sufficient rest. Maintaining good personal health not only helps you to perform well, but it can attract people to you.

In short, when you acquire these work habits, your work performance improves and others' confidence in you increases. Your plan for success calls for you to learn about, as well as carry out, the listed work habits. Over time, while working within a specific environment, you will learn to alter some habits and maintain and improve others.

ASSERTING YOURSELF

Tips for Self-Assessment

- How satisfied am I with my interactions with others?
- To what degree am I willing to stand up for my rights at work?
- How comfortable am I in telling others what I really want them to know?
- To what extent am I willing to give up unassertive behaviors and replace them with assertive ones?
- How can applying assertive behavior in work situations be advantageous to me?

Situations in your work environment may require you to be *assertive*, to stand up for your rights in your behavior with others. Being assertive can be valuable to you, but nagging your co-workers, including the supervisor, will only get you labeled as a pest. Should you experience violations of your rights, carefully evaluate the situation to find out what you can gain and how you can gain it by asserting yourself. Assertive behavior simply means expressing feelings, beliefs, and preferences in a way that is direct, honest, and appropriate. Apparent in your behavior is respect for your own rights as well as for the rights and feelings of co-workers and others.

Nonverbal behavior or body language (eye contact, body movement, tone of voice) is an important part of assertive expression. In assertive behavior, your nonverbal behavior corresponds to what you are saying and, in general, is self-assured, adding strength and emphasis to the words you say. Your voice is appropriately strong. You make eye contact, but do not constantly stare. Your speech sounds expressive and fluent. During appropriate moments it can sound warm or firm. You use body gestures (uses of the hands and head) to further indicate your strength and self confidence.

USING ASSERTIVE BEHAVIOR AT WORK

As you apply assertive behavior in the workplace, strive to improve communication with others and improve your feelings of self-worth. Behave in ways which you will respect, even though your assertive behavior may not always provide what you desire. Additionally, bargain toward workable or equal sharing, as long as bargaining does not detract from or decrease your personal honesty. Using assertive behavior in the workplace can help you feel satisfied with the new position as well as feel good about yourself. After you know that you are accepted, you may offer suggestions, for instance, a change concerning how to approach a certain task. Notice the following examples.

Ineffective: I would like to do more selling in my position.
Effective: I would like to develop a survey to find out what customers think about our products, so that representatives can increase sales.
Ineffective: I don't think that I'm learning new skills in this position.
Effective: I would like to learn more about sketching fashion designs, making experimental pieces of clothing, and marketing decisions.

Generally, you assume your employer or supervisor knows what you should be doing in your position, and he knows of any changes which you should apply. But, after a time, you will know more about your position than anyone else. To attain new responsibilities, you must state in detail what you would like to do, so that your supervisor clearly understands what you have requested. Your employer will likely grant your request, if he does not have to perform background work to determine exactly what you want. Complaining to a supervisor about your position, without specifically stating what changes you seek, places a heavy load on her. She may think, "How can I satisfy this person? What is the person really asking me? What can I do to keep this person quiet? Is this person asking me to . . . ?"

Using assertive behavior clearly tells others what you are requesting. It eliminates any misunderstanding or the need to play *fifty questions* to find out what you want. Using assertive behavior helps you effectively communicate in the workplace.

TYPES OF ASSERTIVE BEHAVIOR

While you should use assertive behavior in the workplace, you must also consider which types of assertive behavior will facilitate good working relationships. Five types of assertive behavior are (a) primary, (b) fellow-feeling, (c) seeking out, (d) I-expression, and (e) heightened.

Tips for Self-Assessment

- Which types of assertive behavior best fit my personality?
- In what situations can my assertive behavior be most effective?

Primary Assertion   You use this type of assertion while standing up for your rights, beliefs, emotions, or opinions. "Are you satisfied with my evaluation of your work performance?" "Yes, I'm satisfied with it." Or, "No, I will not tell a lie for you by punching the clock to show that you arrived on time." Stating "yes" or "no" in an honest way is a primary assertion. Making simple requests, too, indicates a primary assertion. For example, "Bob, how you plan for us to begin the interior design wasn't completely clear to me. Do you mind going over the first stage again?" A primary assertion can include an expression of appreciation, such as "Thank you, Christine, for lending a hand when I really needed one."

Fellow-feeling Assertion   You might use a fellow-feeling assertion in the workplace when you want someone to know you understand their feelings or when you are concerned about how another worker will respond to your assertive behavior. A fellow-feeling assertion includes a statement which recognizes the other worker's feelings, desires, and beliefs as well as a statement which shows you stand up for yourself. Observe the following example: "Mr. Phillips, you really enjoy *happy hour* each day after work, and you feel that I am losing out on a lot of fun. I don't get the same feeling, so I don't believe I'll join you today."

Seeking-out Assertion   This assertion can be appropriate when a difference exists between what another worker has stated he would do and what he really has done. More specifically, a difference occurs between the person's words and his actions. A seeking-out assertion includes an objective description, without blame, of what the worker stated he would do, an objective description of what this person actually did instead, and a statement of what you desire or feel. Examine the following examples. "Sally, I asked you to type up this report for me, and you said that you would get on it within the next five minutes and have it finished in thirty minutes. It is now two hours later, and you have not started. I'd like for you to finish the report." "I gave you permission to use borrow my tools, provided that you would check with me first before taking them. You took some of my tools without letting me know. I want you to explain why you took them without asking."

I-Expression Assertion In a situation where one of your co-worker's behaviors conflicts with yours, you might use an I-expression assertion. You make an objective description, without blame, of the other person's behavior which conflicts with yours, state observable ways in which you are effected, and request the other person to eliminate the conflict. Consider the following example. "Each time we are together, a conflict in attitudes tends to occur. I become upset with you as we converse because you are constantly interrupting me, without allowing me a chance to finish. I want you to respect my feelings and let me say what I have to say before interrupting." Or, "What do you think we can do to avoid this conflict?"

Heightened Assertion You can apply this assertion when your co-worker ignores your first assertion. You might begin with a statement of assertion which will probably cause a slightly negative reaction from a co-worker. As your co-worker continues to ignore what you have stated, your assertive statements become increasingly stronger. A heightened assertion might shift from a simple request to an order or from a statement of choice to a denial. An example of the heightened assertion follows. "I realize that computer programming is difficult for you, and you believe that making a copy of my program will help you improve your chances for a promotion. I'm truly willing to discuss programming with you, but handing my program to you to copy is against my values, and I'd prefer not doing it." . . . "I know that Sal and Bob don't mind sharing their programs. In a way, I want to, but yet I don't." . . . "I've told you that I don't want to do that three times already. I really get upset when you continue pressuring me after I told you no. I refuse to discuss it any further."

Knowledge of only specific career skills is not enough to help you become successful. How you deal with others, including your supervisor or employer, can mean a great deal. Learning to apply the five types of assertive behaviors in appropriate situations will add to your adaptive skills, as discussed in Chapter 6. Using effective assertive behavior in the workplace can produce good work relations and career growth.

HOLDING ON AND LOOKING AHEAD

Tips for Self-Assessment

- Now that I am working, how do I go about holding onto my position?
- What measures can I take to alert myself to the company's decision to lay me off from work or go out of business?
- How might I handle being unemployed?

Now that you have found a position, how do you go about retaining it? Realizing that frequent changes occur in the marketplace, what guarantee do you have that your career skills will remain current throughout your lifespan? These and other questions about career change are important as you consider your position and future advancement. You must continually re-evaluate where you are going.

Say, hypothetically, that you are employed in a position but are concerned with ways to hold onto it as well advance in your career. Do any factors suggest that the company may be on *shaky ground?* Is your workplace losing business, experiencing a falling-off in sales, not rehiring employees for vacant positions, laying off or firing workers, filing for bankruptcy, reorganizing the management and staff, or shifting supervisors into lower level positions? Keep your head out of the sand! Look for these and other situations which warn about the future. Be prepared for the unexpected, so you will be in a position to seek out new career paths. To ignore the warning signs can cripple your career progress. To be aware of the signs, yet not take positive action to correct your situation, is almost as bad. So, identify signs which can work against you, and look for ways to change your work situation. Seek out new employment, contact your employer to clarify existing conditions, or make new contacts to obtain employment information.

Even when no warnings suggest that you seek new employment, keep up-to-date records of your work accomplishments. What new ideas have you introduced to bring about changes in work procedures? On what special projects did you work? For which assignments did you take responsibility? What awards have you received, such as special sales or production recognition? Recording answers to these questions can help you when you try to move up the career ladder, increase your salary, or retain your position, particularly when your employer is considering cutting costs by eliminating employees. When should you enter your accomplishments in your record book? Since you may forget things after a few days have passed, list your achievements as soon as they occur. This method will prevent you from trying to resurrect a task which you may have forgotten or forgetting important details of your work. So, do not wait until later; record your accomplishments now!

Jean Greenwald

It's a good idea to jot down your accomplishments at the close of each work day.

Are you, alone, keeping a record of your accomplishments? If others, such as your employer and supervisor, do not know what you have done, you may not receive full credit. Make a habit of informing others about your accomplishments. If you do not *toot your own horn,* who else will? This does not mean that you should brag about your achievements—you need only to inform others about them.

Learning a variety of work skills will also help you hold on to a position. Try to become aware of which skills apply to other positions. Volunteer to work in another position when a co-worker is absent. By acquiring the skills of another position, you become more valuable to your place of employment. Your initiative can lead to a promotion and/or increase in salary. So, lend a helping hand to co-workers when needed. You can also learn additional skills by attending workshops, in-service meetings, professional seminars, or by requesting your employer to allow you to train for a position which is not yet filled.

Be ready to move to another work environment, should your position fold or a better position await you. Remember, you can do little if you are not prepared. Always consider getting new or up-to-date skills which will allow you to make a career change. You can acquire such skills by attending classes at community colleges, four-year colleges and universities, or post-secondary vocational and technical schools. Educational television courses, correspondence training, state and federal government programs, and military service may also serve as means to additional skills.

Identifying an experienced worker and taking notes from her can mean getting ahead in your career. As the two of you work together, she may give you the kind of encouragement, guidance, and support you need. You will also learn how the system works, where she is within it, and the informal written rules for obtaining a raise or promotion and dealing with co-workers.

Carry out networking to remain aware of available positions. Your business and conference contacts will continue providing a wealth of information about available career opportunities, as well as where to get new career skills. Let everyone you know in your network, especially those who may work for companies hiring persons in your field, that you are seeking career options.

Regularly evaluate your situation to determine which strategies you can use to either hold onto your position, move up the career ladder, or switch to a new position. Remember that career success will largely depend on how much effort you put forth in checking out your situation and in deciding what you should do next. The responsibility is yours!

NINE STEPS TOWARD ACHIEVING A PROMOTION

Tips for Self-Assessment

- What factors make me believe that I deserve a promotion?
- What strengths in my work performance make me think that I deserve an increase in pay?
- Since I perform my work well, to what extent should I rely upon my employer to initiate a promotion and/or pay increase for me?
- What steps might I take to obtain a promotion and salary raise?

Right now you may not be giving much thought to moving in your career and/or gaining an increase in salary, but, at some point, you may consider making more money and heading up the career ladder. When this happens, you might ask yourself, and possibly others around you, such questions as: What do I need to do to get a promotion? I know where I want to go in my career, but how do I get there? I am making a significant contribution to the company by saving them several thousand dollars, but how do I let my employer know that I deserve a salary increase? Although employer and supervisors frequently tell me that I am a good worker, why doesn't my employer increase my salary? You should consider taking the following steps to initiate a promotion.

1. *State your career goal precisely.* Your chances of achieving success increase once you have a clear understanding of your objective.

2. *Envision accomplishing your goal.* Fantasize or daydream about, for example, the rewards of being a supervisor, president, or manager. Each

day, dream that you have achieved your goal. As you dream, enjoy your new office, new career title on your business card, your paycheck with a higher salary, your expanded staff, and the like. As you react to these thoughts, your mind will provide many ideas and hunches to help make these fantasies come true.

3. *Apply the 85/15 rule.* Sharply define what outcomes would assure you a promotion. Then vigorously begin to accomplish them. Each day spend 85 percent of your time on the most important 85 percent of your career, and only 15 percent of your time on the work which provides 15 percent of the bottom-line results. During each of your work activities— writing a report, typing a letter, making a phone call, or programming a computer—ask yourself, "to what extent is this bringing me closer to my goal?"

4. *Increase your visibility as a star performer.* As you think of useful ideas or achieve fantastic results, share them with others by writing a memo. When you attend meetings with your co-workers, be fully prepared. During meetings do not be afraid to communicate your insights. Wherever possible, do not become involved with thankless tasks; instead, take on those where your results will be acknowledged and rewarded.

5. *Engage in risk-taking.* Many workers avoid taking responsibility. Such workers afford you with the chance to move beyond them. Be assertive and take responsibility at every opportunity. You will have much to gain by trying to improve your value to the company.

6. *Extend your career beyond your specialized area.* The single best way to speed up advancement or receive a salary increase is to demonstrate skills outside a specialized area. For example, become a key person, one who has a clear understanding of the total business. Currently you might be earning $18,000 a year as an industrial sales representative, but if you have a basic understanding of the company's general functions and how these functions are associated, you will probably know as much, or more, than most of the senior department managers earning $45,000 to $60,000. Some of them may be locked in their specialized career areas and will lack a broad vision for the company. In this kind of situation, you may well get your chance to advance.

7. *Avoid risking your credibility on false, incomplete, or old information.* You should know all the facts when presenting reports to persons in the workplace. You put your credibility on the line each time you make a written or verbal recommendation. Therefore, always use up-to-date, complete, and reliable information. Your co-workers will view you as an impressive performer when you present useful facts and figures.

8. *Be the first to identify business trends which can affect the company.* One way to advance ahead of your co-workers is to alert your company of opportunities or pitfalls which the changing economic climate may cause. You need to be alert to possible developments before they actually happen.

You should know more than *what* is going to occur, but *why* it will happen. Try to explain the connections between new facts and ongoing issues and patterns. Having this kind of information gives you greater understanding of how to take advantage of major changes in your company. This step requires you to read newspapers, magazines, and books and to talk to persons knowledgeable about current and upcoming business trends.

9. *Learn from other workers' experiences.* You can learn from the successes and failures of other professionals. How can you get this information? Well, you may talk to others, observe others' actions, and read life stories (autobiographies and biographies) of interesting persons whose career is similar to yours. Taking advantage of their strategies to attain success and avoid failures.

In short, the responsibility for advancement is yours. If you apply the suggested nine steps, you may improve your situation. Work with these steps in mind as you attempt to move up the career ladder and increase your salary.

MAINTAINING CAREER SATISFACTION

Tips for Self-Assessment

- How can I make my career a continually satisfying experience?
- What kinds of ongoing features must a career provide to meet my needs?
- How much effort should I make to identify and meet requirements and needs of my employer and co-workers?

You will remain satisfied with your career only when persons at your workplace frequently reward your efforts and when you, in turn, offer your employer your best job performance. In other words, you and your workplace must meet each other's needs. Your employer will feel satisfied with your work when she sees you being on time, handling co-workers diplomatically, presenting creative ideas, helping solve problems, taking pride in your job, turning out quality work, or furthering the development of the workplace. Your employer provides you with a salary and raises, profit sharing, promotions, paid health and life insurance, vacations, awards and formal recognition, use of a company car, and verbal feedback through an understanding supervisor. How long will you remain satisfied with your present position? If you are generally satisfied with your position, will you feel satisfied each working day? Most persons would like to wake up each morning eager to face new career challenges, but that is not the case for many of us. Your initial enthusiasm may not last, and you may feel dissatisfied with your position much of the time, even though you generally like it. What might contribute to your displeasure? Some examples of factors which lead to career dissatisfaction are the following:

routine work tasks	little personal worth at work
lack of employee cooperation	inability to do tasks well
no or low salary increases	supervisory criticism
few opportunities to learn new tasks	employee rules
poor health conditions	travel requirements
boring work tasks	organizational change
little, if any, personal recognition	limited parking space
hazardous working conditions	few fringe benefits

How you handle these and other factors will determine your length of service and your level of performance. Continually evaluate your situation to discover how satisfied you feel in your position. Identify these preceding factors so that you can act on them as they begin to occur, rather than dealing with them later. An interesting question to ask yourself, too, is "How well am I meeting the needs of the workplace?" You may be satisfied with the workplace, but your employer may be dissatisfied with your job performance. The relationship between you and the workplace should be a *total love affair!*

AVOIDING DISTRESS

Tips for Self-Assessment

- How easily do I become anxious or tense due to time pressures, work frustrations, or arguments?
- How do these factors affect my work performance?
- How should I handle stressful factors which might weaken my work performance?

Many factors which cause you to be dissatisfied with your position can also result in your experiencing personal stress. Stress occurs when you feel threatened or feel inadequate in a particular situation. Often you may experience a certain degree of stress. Many physicians believe dealing with some stress is beneficial, but when you endure stress over long periods it becomes *distress*—a negative stress. Distress, the obvious showing of unusually high stress levels, can occur when you are experiencing high anxiousness or tenseness, time pressures, work frustrations, anger due to arguments, or any type of continued stress. You may experience a negative physical reaction to stress. Observe the following example.

> The afternoon is nearly half over, and Ms. Stein must complete four or five work tasks—finish a brief report, conduct a staff meeting, read and sign some papers, and phone the district manager. At this point Ms. Stein doesn't think she can finish her work in any kind of organized way. On this afternoon, like many other afternoons, she is tense and frustrated, due to her predicament.

This example suggests that Ms. Stein is experiencing some degree of distress—her stress level has mounted over time because she continues to approach each day without sensing any relief at work. What should she do to avoid her distress? First, she must learn to set priorities. Ms. Stein must begin asking herself, "Which tasks can I afford to postpone until tomorrow?" Possibly if she postpones several tasks, she can immediately decrease her frustration and tenseness. For instance, now that she feels no rush to arrive at and conduct the meeting, she no longer feels a great deal of unwanted pressure. Often you find yourself having too much work to do. If you are energetic and set high career goals for yourself, you will often have more to do than you may be able to complete. Understanding and pacing yourself will help you set priorities. By prioritizing you can reduce time pressure, a common cause of distress.

Each day you will face stressful factors. Some of them are less noticeable than others, but you will best handle them if you can pick them out. Be aware of the following list of such factors.

1. *Time pressures*—Daily, you may be trying to do more than you are able; attempting to accomplish much in little time. You become tense when you fail to meet your goals, and you may also waste time by working haphazardly on many tasks.

2. *Career frustration*—You may become upset when things are "just not going well at the shop" or when your supervisor does not know what you are attempting to do. Review your situation at work, and try to resolve any difficulties which might arise by discussing them with your supervisor or co-workers before the difficulties mount. Allow others to express their views, but be sure to get your point across clearly and positively.

3. *Rigid company structures*—When you are unable to communicate directly with company policymakers, you may feel frustrated. If you do attempt to follow company policy by communicating through your immediate supervisor, he may repeat your information incorrectly, and you are left feeling misundertood and tense. Still, you might consider examining the policies and rules of the company, initiating a positive dialogue with your employer or supervisor to explain the difficulties inherent in the present structure, and, if possible, offer suggestions to improve the work environment.

4. *Waiting on others*—Waiting on co-workers to complete their portion of joint tasks can often cause you to become restless. You might try two different methods to avoid this frustration. First, if possible, encourage co-workers to reschedule their tasks so both of you can prevent wasting valuable company time. Second, if you cannot avoid waiting, encourage pleasant feelings while you wait. Fill your waiting time by planning and organizing your next tasks, or work on other projects.

5. *Family illness*—Tensions concerning serious family illness lead to sincere distress among family members. Frequently, an elderly family member must suffer through a serious illness. Other family members must address this situation and plan a course of action to ease the tension.

6. *Everyday boredom*—Boredom often causes stress which, in turn, leads to unfilled needs and worry. Work needs to be full of variety and challenge. If you seldom experience these feelings at work, then you should pursue leisure activities outside the workplace. Integrate the activities into each day to break any monotony you may be experiencing.

7. *Deadlines*—Deadlines can be an unnoticed stress factor. Sometimes deadlines we establish for ourselves are worse than those made by others. Deadlines help you meet your objectives. Used properly, they signal that you must complete certain tasks before moving toward broader goals. Try to be realistic as you set time limits, so you will not cause delays; however, avoid setting limits which disrupt a smooth operation of work.

8. *Work addiction*—When you prefer working at your career more than other activities, including your family and leisure involvements, you may be *addicted* to work. Some psychologists theorize that a person addicted to work experiences tension during his leisure activities. Taking on large amounts of work; staying at the shop, office, or store for additional hours each day; or even bringing work home at night or on weekends will not necessarily increase your output. Your inability, or refusal, to function in a variety of activities may cause you to take a less active approach to work over time. To reduce addiction to work, participate in a variety of leisure activities.

9. *Disorganization*—Disorganization, the inability to find needed things or regain information on short notice, may cause unnecessary tension. Planning ahead enables you to arrange and set up those tasks which require your immediate attention. Planning allows you to feel comfortable because you understand which direction you are headed and how you can achieve your goals.

10. *Flawlessness*—Along with using time unwisely, needing to produce the highest quality work can also lead to stress. You may often waste energy and cause yourself anger while attempting to produce flawless work, when in fact, such work may not be required. To eliminate this attitude, set reasonable work standards and strive to meet them. After you achieve the standard, go directly to the next task.

11. *Work/family problems*—Relationships with the people in your family (wife, children, parents) and those at work (supervisor, employer, co-workers) can be important elements in your life. Conflict in either, or both, of these relationships may lead to distress. You occasionally need to re-evaluate your relationships to determine if friction could be triggering your discomfort.

12. *Worrying about unchangeables*—No doubt, you have enough concerns without worrying about things which you cannot change. Such things are the *unchangeables*. Unchangeable events or factors are inherent in most workplaces. Learn to accept many of these, and spend your time on factors which you can control.

13. *Delaying tasks for later*—Delaying work until a later time can make you feel anxious about tasks which you need to finish. Developing

goals for both your leisure activities and career serves as a blueprint for you to follow. When you say, "I really should . . . ," you are delaying portions of your work. Reduce your stress by completing those tasks which you feel are most important.

14. *Unknown events*—Worrying about uncertain events concerning your career or future can contribute to stress. Your work itself may cause you stress if you are familiar with everything that goes on there. Remaining unaware of certain information about the workplace (bankruptcy, layoffs, firings, promotions) can cause you to become anxious. You can reduce much of the uncertainty occurring in the workplace by initiating a dialogue with your employer, supervisor, and/or co-workers.

In short, much of what goes on in your workplace or home can lead to undue stress and eventually distress. Avoid such things as dreaming about a production quota or worrying about your shortcomings, a pay raise, or a promotion. Do not miss needed sleep at night because of your work shift. Do not over-react to your supervisor's harsh criticisms. Try to put marital problems or family illnesses in proper perspective. How well you handle such situations will, in part, determine your career success.

FUTURE CONSIDERATIONS

Tips for Self-Assessment

- What is my present career goal?
- How might this career goal change during my lifespan?
- Although I am currently satisfied, what strategies should I keep in mind to effectively change my career when the time comes?

Should you plan to attain the highest career available within a specific field? The answer is *yes* for some of us. For others, career paths which include lateral or downward moves within a work setting or moves to new locations, providing career enrichment or opportunity, may be more suitable. Certainly, strive for a position which corresponds to your needs and interests, as well as the available opportunities within a work environment.

Should you cease building your career once you have attained an immediate goal? The answer is *no!* To a large extent, factors outside your control influence your original career decision. Such factors may cause you to reevaluate your plans many times. For example, you may become interested in a newly created career; you may be temporarily, or permanently, laid off your job; your changing physical or mental abilities may induce you to switch careers; a changeover in machinery or work procedures may force you to learn new skills; or a merger or bankruptcy might eliminate your current position.

Even after reaching your first major goal, continue making future career plans. Prepare for opportunities within your current work setting or elsewhere. By continually planning, you can better determine your career future and lessen the influence of external events. If your career path becomes blocked by obstacles which prevent you from attaining a sought-after goal, plan alternative paths. After working in a chosen field, many persons find that striving for *the top* is not worth it. They find that a high-level career, such as supervisor, manager, accountant, airline pilot, public school administrator, retail proprietor, or foreman, is not what they wanted. Once having experienced top level careers, some workers are unwilling to endure the demands, responsibilities, emotional stress, and headaches sometimes associated with them. Other workers reconsider their goals when their present career does not provide them with self-satisfaction, creative work experiences, opportunities for personal growth, or sufficient time with their families. Before you make a vertical move to a position requiring more or different job skills, follow these three steps: (a) identify your reason(s) for wanting to make an upward career move, (b) examine your personal values (interests, likes, and dislikes) in relation to the desired career, and (c) explore the demands and responsibilities of the new career by interviewing persons in the career and reading about it.

DECIDING TO MAKE A LATERAL CAREER MOVE

For one reason or another, many of us want to make a career move, but we are not interested in a career having higher status, a position having a larger salary, or a job where we must handle more responsibility. Instead, we consider making a lateral move, to increase work skills, to learn new skills which are not required in our present career, to attain a broader knowledge of our work setting, or to prepare ourselves in the event that our present position may be phased out. For example, Don makes a lateral move from an insurance salesperson to an automobile insurance claims adjuster. Through this move he will learn how to evaluate clients' auto-mobile claims. He will transfer his old skills and acquire new ones.

Before making a lateral move, investigate the attitudes within your present work environment toward such career changes. Determine if the general atmosphere encourages lateral moves. Next, identify and locate sources of information—personnel directors, career specialist, co-workers, as well as in-house publications and posted career announcements. Check out leads for in-house lateral moves. Finally, identify and then examine the new work environment and its corresponding benefits before making a lateral career move.

STEPPING DOWN THE CAREER LADDER

Many persons have never considered, let alone moved to, a lower-level career. Yet, many become *fed up* with frustrations, stress, and the over-whelming responsibilities which often go along with high-status careers. In some instances, persons opt for a lower-level career—moving down the career ladder to less salary and status, but also to greater career satisfaction, peace of mind, opportunity for creativity, and fewer responsibilities.

Changing positions from an elementary school principal to a sixth-grade classroom teacher or from a computer programmer to a data processor are examples of such career moves. You might find an upper-level career beyond your ability and consider moving to a lower-level career within your present work setting. Before making a decision to step down the career ladder, take the following actions.

1. Start by evaluating why you feel the need to switch to a lower-level career.
2. Clarify your values and lifestyle in relation to one or more lower-level career options available to you.
3. Conduct personal interviews with co-workers within your present work setting who have made a downward career change.
4. Gather and examine information from various sources (neighbors; community, state and federal agencies; newspapers; and pamphlets) about the personal reactions of workers who have made a downward career choice.
5. Investigate the attitudes and policies within your present work setting toward downward career change.
6. Contact your personnel director and determine the effects on your compensation, should you switch to a lower-level career.

LEAVING YOUR PRESENT WORK ENVIRONMENT

You may find that at some point (six months, one or two years, etc.) your career is unsuited to your needs. For example, you may feel that you are not being awarded a promotion which you rightly deserve, that you are being underpaid, or that your salary will not increase significantly. Perhaps your position does not meet your personal needs, or the supervisory personnel at your present place of employment find your work performance less than they desire.

Two basic choices are available to you. Consider altering your present work situation, or consider moving to a different work environment. The first choice may entail the following steps:

1. Identify and explore your reasons for wanting to change your present work environment.
2. Determine and eliminate unrealistic reasons.
3. Investigate alternatives within your present work setting to improve your career (acquiring new computer skills, performing new tasks, or accepting greater responsibility).
4. Consider updating your skills by attending a class at a community college or an in-house training program.
5. Approach your supervisor, or other personnel, concerning possibilities for improving your career skills or present position.

The second alternative, moving to a different work environment, may be the only choice open to you. Having that choice in mind, consider the following:

1. Explore your reasons for wanting to move to another work setting.
2. Investigate all possible career alternatives in your present work setting.
3. If no career alternatives exist, define steps for securing employment at another workplace.
4. Determine whether or not you wish to remain in the same career field or switch to another.
5. If you decide to switch career fields, identify which field you should enter and explore methods which appear most feasible in attaining your new goal (for example, going to the local community college part-time or full-time versus attending seminars and workshops.)
6. If you decide to remain in your career field, identify and begin speaking with informed sources about potential work settings (for example, personal contacts, career development specialists, and employment agencies).
7. Explore and evaluate your career options.
8. Consider only options which will help you achieve your career goals.

SEARCHING FOR OTHER POTENTIAL CAREERS

While you may not be convinced that a career move is suitable for you, consider avenues which might help you retain options. Your planning is never complete without forethought of possible events. Unpredictable occurrences can make a rigid career plan worthless. Thus, career planning means preparing for upcoming changes.

To improve your ongoing chances in the marketplace, consider modifying your goals (when needed) and exploring aspects of other career fields, as well as your own. To stay abreast of new information and update your skills, (a) seek interviews with workers whose career fields are different from yours to learn about responsibilities and required skills in their fields; (b) attend local, state, and national professional organizations' annual meetings, seminars, and workshops; (c) attend in-house workshops and professional development seminars; (d) read journal articles and books to broaden your knowledge of career fields; (e) concentrate your attention on one career field at a time; (f) explore your career goals in relationship to each field; and (g) discover what career positions are available.

Career decision making is not a one-shot procedure but something you should consider throughout your lifetime. Generally, when a person is undecided about a particular career, she seeks assistance. The same person might also require assistance later while considering a career change.

You might have based your initial career selection on a sudden fancy, having only inaccurate information or limited career options. Anyone can choose a career, but only a few persons have learned the process of intelligent career selection.

No single career will always be best for you. Unknown life events can affect your entry into a particular field. Therefore, periodically clarify and re-evaluate your interests, values, and lifestyles. While at your job, learn from new experiences. Ask yourself, "Does this career give me what I now desire?" and "Will this career continue providing challenges for me?"

POINTS TO REVIEW

1. The first day of work can be an important experience. How you prepare and respond to this new challenge may determine your succeess in days to come. Remember, the first day of the rest of your career life begins with the impression you make on your employer and/or supervisor and co-workers. Focus your attention on work, but do not forget to be friendly.

2. Learning the accepted behavior of a new position will help you make a good start. Ask experienced co-workers to tell you about work policies, to share methods for improving your work, and how to deal cooperatively with others.

3. In most new career situations, expect to gain professional training, work experience, credentials, visual exposure, and contact. Some positions will provide these and other factors better than others.

4. Develop your personal qualities, such as dependability, efficiency, drive, honesty, consideration, respectfulness, orderliness, time management, and personal health, until they become part of your daily work behavior.

5. As you work with others, use assertive behavior. Express your feelings, beliefs, and preferences in a way that is direct, honest, and gives high regard for your rights, as well as for the rights and feelings of co-workers and others.

6. Five types of assertive behaviors will help you develop good working relationships with your supervisor and co-workers: (a) primary, (b) fellow-feeling, (c) seeking-out, (d) I-expression, and (e) heightened. Applying these behaviors in appropriate situations will add to your adaptive skills.

7. Being prepared for an unexpected career change allows you to react to situations early enough to seek out new career paths; ignoring the warning signs can lessen your career options.

8. To protect your career future, consider the following: (a) record your accomplishments, (b) learn a variety of work skills, (c) be ready to move

to another work environment, (d) work closely with an experienced co-worker to gain information, and (e) participate in ongoing networking.

9. In order for you to feel satisfied at work, your employer must reward you for your skills and services, and you must reward him for the pay and benefits which you receive. Yet, many factors lead to job dissatisfaction. How you handle these factors will determine your success within a certain workplace.

10. Several factors leading to personal stress and eventually distress are (a) time pressures, (b) career frustration, (c) rigid company structures, (d) waiting on others, (e) family illness, (f) boredom, (g) deadlines, (h) work addiction, (i) disorganization, (j) seeking perfection, (k) unchangeables, (l) task delays, and (m) unknown events.

Experiential Exercises

1. Hazel has just been hired as sales supervisor of women's clothing for a large department store located in an urban area. Describe what Hazel might expect to gain from her new position with reference to the following items:

   Professional training

   Work experience

   Credentials

   Visible exposure

   Professional contacts

2. John will complete his program next month in automobile body repair at St. Mary's Community College. He has been offered a position at Perry's Mercedes Benz Imports. John is seriously considering the position but is also comparing it with a Cadillac dealership. Describe what comparisons you think John should make before choosing one position over the other.

3. Effective work habits are crucial to your success. Assume that you are now working in your desired position. Evaluate the personal qualities you demonstrate to your employer and co-workers. (After recording your evaluations, consider how you would strengthen any weaknesses in each area.)

   Dependability

   Efficiency

Drive

Honesty

Consideration

Respectfulness

Orderliness

Time Management

Personal Health

4. Applying assertive behavior in the workplace will help you feel satisfied with your new position, as well as help you feel satisfied about yourself. The following exercises give you experience in identifying and applying assertive behavior. Determine whether each of the statements is effective or ineffective assertive behavior. Then describe your reasons for each choice.

a. *Pointing out unsatisfactory work performance*

Statement 1. "Bill, you're really inadequate as a drill press operator. If this is how you are going to perform, we might as well forget it right now. I could get more satisfaction by doing it myself."

Statement 2. "Bill, I'd like to talk to you about improving your work on the drill press, so that you can turn out a more satisfactory product. For one thing, I think you need to slow down so that you can drill the holes in proper places."

Which statement is more effective? Why?

b. *Refusing a co-worker's request to borrow tools*

Statement 3. "Absolutely not! I've had enough of your leeching tools off me."

Statement 4. "I'm sorry, but the last time you borrowed my tools, you were careless with them and got them greasy. I don't want to lend my tools to you anymore."

Which statement is the more effective? Why?

c. *Refusing a supervisor's request to work overtime*

Statement 5. "No thanks, Mr. Brown! You couldn't pay me enough to work overtime tonight. Why don't you try working on the report yourself?"

Statement 6. "Mr. Brown, I'm sorry, but I feel too tired to work tonight after working on the report all day. I do hope you can find someone else."

Which statement is the more effective? Why?

5. You often need to use assertive behavior to achieve your career goals. Give an example of *how* or *when* you could use each of the following assertive behaviors while on the job.
   Primary Assertion

   Fellow-Feeling Assertion

   Seeking-Out Assertion

   I-Expression Assertion

   Heightened Assertion

6. Say that you have landed a new position as an automobile claims adjuster. Although you enjoy your work, you must be alert to warning signs which suggest negative factors about your new position.
   a. List factors which could change your present career course.

   b. Describe factors which suggest you should hold onto your position and/or move ahead in your chosen career.

7. To remain satisfied with your career, you need to feel good about your workplace. Evaluate factors about your place of work to determine which ones you wish to change or deal with more fully. Use the following list as an evaluation tool. You may add other factors to this list which fit your particular work setting. Place a check mark ($\sqrt{}$) opposite each work factor indicating how you feel about it.

Workplace Characteristics	Very Satisfied	Satisfied	Uncertain	Dissatisfied	Very Dissatisfied
Salary/Wages					
Promotion procedure					
Business travel					
Company policies					
Benefits					
Weather					
Inside temperature					
Work area					
Vacations					
Parking facilities					
Security of work environment					
Ventilation					
Travel distance to and from work					
Lighting					
Quality of sound					
Time off for illness					
Personal time off					
Eating facilities					
Work supplies					
Janitorial service					
Lunch period					
Break period					
Appearance of work area					
Company or office organization					
Distractions					
Other:					

8. Examine the check marks you have placed alongside the workplace characteristics. Review the characteristics you have marked with *dissatisfied* and *very dissatisfied* evaluations. List ways you could make improvements.

9. The quality of the relationships between persons within your workplace can affect your level of satisfaction. Rate the quality of your relationships in the workplace by placing a check mark ($\sqrt{}$) in the appropriate spaces.

Workers	Very Satisfied	Satisfied	Uncertain	Dissatisfied	Very Dissatisfied
Supervisor(s)					
Employer					
Co-workers					
Management officials					
Secretaries					
Committee members					
Clients/customers					
Janitorial staff					
Personnel staff					
Your support staff					
President					
Union officials					
Union organization					
Apprentice or intern					
Mentor					
Workers in other businesses					
Others:					

10. List those workers whom you have rated in the *dissatisfied* or *very dissatisfied* groups. Next, identify the problems in your relationship and list them next to the worker. Consider strategies you might use to improve the quality of the relationship, and record them after the workers and identified problems.

Workers: *Problems in Your Relationships:*

a.

b.

c.

d.

e.

f.

Strategies to Improve a Relationship:

a.

b.

c.

d.

e.

f.

11. Many times, career dissatisfaction results from your own thoughts and behavior, rather than from the workplace or other workers. Examine the following list and mark which factors are working toward your career dissatisfaction.

Personal Concerns	No	Yes
Getting to work on time		
Worrying about personal illness		
Worrying about family illness		
Worrying about personal stress		
Adapting to change		
Maintaining good attendance record		
Adapting to new situations		
Taking responsibility		
Following company policies		
Being interested in outside activities		
Maintaining personal drive		
Willingness to take risks		
Acting cooperatively		
Approaching work in a business-like manner		
Showing interest in job tasks and/or co-workers		

12. Review only the preceding items which concern *you*. List those items and identify possible reasons why each is a concern. Then write methods you might use to alleviate your concerns.

Personal Concerns: *Reasons for Concern:*

a.

b.

c.

d.

Methods to Alleviate Concerns

a.

b.

c.

d.

13. Imagine that you have gotten a position in your preferred career, and you want to move up the career ladder. Describe the steps you would take to make this vertical move.

14. Assume that you have been working on a career for the past four years and want to make a lateral move within your present work environment. Describe the steps you would take to make this lateral move.

15. Suppose you found yourself in a career which required skills beyond your abilities. List information you might seek before moving down the career ladder.

16. Pretend that you have been working in a career for three years but find your work environment unsuited to your needs. Describe options which are available to you.

C H A P T E R

9

It is better to prepare for the future now than to wait until you get there.

Lifelong Planning

In earlier chapters we have outlined ideas for preparing for career entry, holding onto a position, and moving up the career ladder. Should these steps be the extent of career planning? "Yes," according to twenty-eight year old Julie. "After all," she says, "I am working, my family and I are satisfied, and I see myself moving up the career ladder quite soon—what could go wrong?" Julie's perception of career planning is not necesarily accurate. Career planning is not simply a matter of avoiding problems, but rather, learning how to react to the work environment, which will likely change. Career planning should not be a single life event. Instead, it is an ongoing, systematic approach for examining alternatives, as well as recognizing barriers which could interfere with making a satisfactory choice. As indicated throughout this book, career planning extends throughout your life, as you continually make decisions about your career and related activities.

A useful career plan requires that you frequently determine what changes are taking place in your life. For example, you may ask yourself such questions as, "How do my interests, values, or lifestyle differ from (or resemble) those which I had ten years ago? How will the attributes which I now have change fifteen years hence? Will these changes affect my work performance? Will I be as alert in twenty years as I am now?" In point, you must not lose sight of how personal changes or societal changes will alter your job status.

This chapter describes how you may assess your career development in terms of where you are today and where you may be going later in life. To assess your career status, you will need to evaluate changes as they occur. How you approach each stage of your career and what takes place during each stage is important. Your psychological development also influences how you deal with your career, family, friends, co-workers, and yourself.

Generally, adulthood is the longest portion of a person's life. Yet, few adults look beyond their present stage to determine what actions, if any, they need to take to ensure a later satisfactory lifestyle. Moving through each stage of development generally increases an individual's maturity. This maturity does not necessarily occur upon entry into early adulthood, but develops as each of us deals with changes or tasks in each new life stage.

Adult career development can be divided into three broad categories, early adulthood, middle adulthood, and late adulthood.[1] We will examine each of these stages in ten-year intervals in order to help you identify where you may be now and see what might occur within your lifetime.

EARLY ADULTHOOD (20–40 YEARS OF AGE)

Young adults begin establishing a viable career. Their behavior is initially characterized by a need to make a commitment to consistent work involvement. Their work behavior also includes characteristics such as reality testing, self-discovery, skill development and refinement, building interpersonal relationships, and the need to plan for a career.

AGE SPAN 20–30

Tips for Self-Assessment

- Am I choosing a particular career just for a high salary? If so, how will my salary help me reach at least one of my goals?
- Will this career allow me to provide for the needs of a family?
- Will my career permit me to enter social circles which I would like to be a part of in ten years?

[1]Jeffrey S. Turner and Donald B. Helms, *Contemporary Adulthood* (Philadelphia, PA: W. B. Sanders, 1979).

The type and amount of formal education you attain and the values of your parents, teachers, and peers most influence you during this age span. Young adults generally become more independent in thought and action as parental influence lessens and peer influence increases. Many young adults leave their family and start living on their own.

Courtship, marriage, adjusting to married life, rearing children, participating in civic activities, and developing social relationships all crowd the early years of this age span. Yet, many women are now delaying marriage and are first attaining professional and upper-level managerial careers. Some couples marry and opt for dual careers and child rearing, while other dual career couples do not even consider parenting. The realities of life become more important as young adults start a career, begin professional training, and attempt to develop a self-identity.

The younger persons of this group may or may not recognize the need to plan their careers. If a person does commit himself to a career field, he first finds a position and tries out a potential career. When young adults make a career commitment, they are predicting how well they will adjust to and remain satisfied with a particular field. If their predictions are inaccurate, and they do not make a satisfactory personal adjustment, they may change careers, move to another work environment, or enter school for new or improved skills.

During this period, some persons will immediately decide to begin a career without having explored available options and opportunities. Others may remain undecided about which career to select. The latter group may well enter low-paying work and move from one kind of job to the next.

Ages twenty-five to thirty are transitional years, connecting early and middle adulthood. At this time persons may decide that the career field they originally chose is unsatisfactory, and they may make one or two career changes before discoveirng a more satisfactory life goal. Increasing numbers of women and men are entering, or re-entering, postsecondary schools during this period to gain career skills before entering a new career. For some this preparation may precede as much as the fifth career change.[2] Such persons' career changes may occur for a variety of reasons: loss of spouse or work, family's financial need, change in lifestyle, availability of new career opportunities, or personal fulfillment. For whatever reason, young adults begin to show a need to have a firm career role. As a result, they become better able to handle the subsequent changes in their career development. Sometimes, persons may find a suitable career after working in a succession of unrelated positions. Frequently, in this age span, persons begin preparing for long-range commitments as well as for making a maximum contribution at their work. They may prepare to move to a new position or employment setting. An individual may deal with feelings of achievement and/or failure in her initial career, learn to accept subordinate

[2]Jerry L. Davis and Roy B. Hackman, "Vocational Adjustment: Prevention or Correction Emphasis?" in *Human Behavior in a Changing Society*, ed. J. Adams (Boston, MA: Holbrook Press, 1973), 213–221.

Jean Greenwald

Younger workers often seek the advice of a *mentor*.

status, or learn how to get along with the employer/supervisor and with peers.

Often, workers in their twenties closely follow the advice and practice of a *mentor,* a seasoned or more experienced worker in the same workplace. The relationship between the two (young worker and mentor) provides the younger person with a sense of security and builds his self-confidence. The mentor helps the young worker acquire needed information about the ins and outs of the specific work environment and may also help him refine skills, obtain promotions, and earn raises. While the mentor is likely to be of the same sex as the young worker, young women, working in what were once male-dominated fields, often choose male mentors.

AGE SPAN 30–40

Tip for Self-Assessment

- How committed am I to becoming a *professional* in my chosen career?
- As a woman, which is more important—a career or a family?
- Should a *two-paycheck family* consider rearing children?

Career behaviors which begin in a person's twenties often overlap with those which occur during his early thirties. For most individuals, ages thirty-one to forty-four are creative years. Due to advantages (or barriers) in the work environment, persons may reevaluate their earlier decisions. Self-

© Linda Ammons

With more job experience, you gain the sense of *being your own person.*

questioning of achievements and of career direction often describe this age span. Some persons may feel disillusioned about their career and life status. Factors which offered persons direction in their twenties seem to provide little direction as they strive to meet new goals. Thus, persons may experience some degree of turmoil. Resolving such feelings generally results in a restored sense of balance. Persons may reaffirm an earlier lifestyle and career choice or make new choices. The thirty through forty age span is followed by a period of stabilization, which often includes such behavior as *settling down* within a specific career field and applying talents suitable to a career choice.

During the *settling down* period, as suggested by Levinson and his associates,[3] the individual strives to achieve two major tasks.

1. To establish a niche in society: to dig in; anchor his (or her) life more firmly; develop competence in a chosen craft; become a valued member of a valued world.

[3]Daniel J. Levinson et al., *The Seasons of Man's Life* (New York: Alfred A. Knopf, 1978).

2. To work at 'making it': planning, striving to advance, progressing along a timetable.[4]

The term *making it,* used broadly, includes efforts to establish a better life, to obtain goals valued by society, to contribute to society, and to receive recognition from it. In short, the term implies advancement up the career ladder. Your tasks in the settling down period will be to become a fulfilled adult and to define a lifelong plan of self-direction.

Levinson and his associates[5] explain that near the end of this period, generally around thirty-six or thirty-seven, a person may exprience the sense of *being one's own person.* An individual states specifically what she desires, although she may or may not actually obtain it. During this time she may feel a stronger desire to speak for herself, to become a senior member or expert in her career field, and to have a stronger sense of authority. She may sense that she has not achieved enough, that she is not sufficiently her own person, that others are blocking her accomplishments, and that she is restrained by her own conflicts and inhibitions.

An individual going through this period may also experience the need to cut his ties with a once admired mentor, although this action may be a mentally painful process. An individual may have outgrown the idea of being the protege of an older worker and need to be considered a senior adult, a peer to his mentor and employer. Now begins the time for him to consider his own abilities and interest in becoming a mentor, constructive advisor, and friend to other workers.

MIDDLE ADULTHOOD
40–60 YEARS OF AGE

The period ranging from age thirty-five to sixty-five is marked by physiological and psychological changes. The late thirties or early forties are for most persons the ages during which difficulties occur. Some authorities refer to this phase as the *midlife crisis* or *midcourse correction.*[6] The intensity of this crisis of the late thirties may be influenced by how successfully an individual has dealt with earlier conflicts. As persons move toward the middle adult stage of development (the transitional period betwen early and middle adult stages), they often experience some discomfort.

AGE SPAN 40–50

Levinson[7] suggests that the movement from early adulthood toward middle adulthood should be labeled *midlife transition.* This phase of adult devel-

---

[4]Daniel J. Levinson, "The Mid-Life Transition: A Period in Adult Psychosocial Development," *Psychiatry,* 40 (October 1977): 104.

[5]Levinson, *Seasons of Life,* 144–145.

[6]John S. Dacey, *Adult Development* (Glenview, IL: Scott, Foresman, 1982), 172–173.

[7]Levinson, "The Mid-Life Transition," 107.

opment occurs approximately from ages forty to forty-five. Some doubting and searching are a part of this re-evaluation period, and the results of the re-evaluation may be in opposition to family members or persons in the work environment. On the other hand, one may also receive support from others as he seeks change and self-improvement. He may experience disillusionment with career achievements or marital status. Faced with disappointment, grief, or loss, he may make new realizations.

According to Gail Sheehy,[8] one's personal energies, rather than being directed on external goals or ideas, are directed inward toward one's self. Persons may become more aware of their physical presence and of new aches and pains.

As a result, the middle-aged person becomes more preoccupied with signs of aging and premature failure. This self-awareness can cause her to question her early dreams and goals and her actual achievements and fulfillments.[9] Eric Rayner describes this midlife crises.

> It may be acute, with depression and anxiety, but it is more likely to be quiet. It may even be enjoyable, for change means variety and the opportunity for exploration. An individual is not likely to pinpoint the crisis, for it probably occurs in stages over a period of years. It may be linked with external circumstances like change in work, but it is more likely to be private and internal.[10]

Gail Sheehy[11] states that women begin their midlife phase earlier than men, somewhere around thirty-five, as they start their *last chance*. Whatever women sense they must do as a last chance will depend upon their individual life pattern. Turner and Helms[12] believe a combination of factors contribute to this feeling of *deadline* around age thirty-five, for example, (a) school attendance for the last child, (b) the average age for women to return to the career marketplace, (c) the age when many women leave home, (d) the age when the biological end to childbearing is closer, and (e) the average age for divorced women to re-marry. As these factors occur, many women shift to a midlife perception. Whether they respond to their re-evaluation during this stage, or whether their spouse becomes involved in this process, can vary.

As difficult as middle adulthood can be for men, it is probably even harder for women. According to Alan Knox,[13] ninety percent of women age thirty-five to forty do not have a college degree. Additionally, three-fourths of them do not have a husband or have a mate whose income is in the lower half of incomes in the United States. At this stage the vast majority of divorced women marry for the second time. Also, thirty-five years of age is average for those women who desert their families.

[8]Gail Sheehy, *Passages: Predictable Crises of Adult Life* (New York: Doubleday, 1974).

[9]Turner and Helms, *Contemporary Adulthood*, 109.

[10]Eric Rayner, *Human Development* (London: George Allen and Irwin, 1971), 232.

[11]Sheehy, *Passages*, 392.

[12]Turner and Helms, *Contemporary Adulthood*, 110.

[13]Alan Knox, *Adult Development and Learning* (San Francisco: Jossey-Bass, 1978).

Many adults during the age span of forty to fifty express concern for the differences between their earlier career aspirations and their actual attainments. As a result, many, particularly men, are dissatisfied with their career. They question whether they made the right career moves and if they still have time to make a career change. Robert E. Campbell and James V. Cellini give several reasons for midlife career change.

> People change careers for a variety of reasons. The combination of motives varies somewhat with the individual by sex, age, socioeconomic status, and self-perception, and can be categorized into two broad groups—extrinsic factors and intrinsic factors. Extrinsic factors consist of forces and events external to the person, which precipitate career changes. Work environment, organizational policies, job layoffs, family circumstances, illness, disability, economic conditions, job opportunities, technological changes, and occupational obsolescence are examples of extrinsic factors. Intrinsic factors are internal, behavioral forces within the individual, typically including lifestyle preference, work values and attitudes, achievement motivation, career expectations, personal assessment, risk taking, occupational identity, role conflict, personal reward system, and monotony. Extrinsic and intrinsic factors are not mutually exclusive but, rather, interacting: that is, extrinsic events and intrinsic events are co-variant, producing change decisions. For instance, a major external event like divorce may stimulate internal personal reassessment and career redirection.[14]

Some major social patterns shaping midlife self-reevaluation and career switching are influences of the women's movement and more women establishing careers; technological advancement (or a changing economy) causing careers to reach a dead-end prematurely; unemployment at middle age; worker's longer lifespan; changes in educational needs; and a decreasing notion that one should have a lifelong career.[15]

Which middle-aged persons change careers? Robert E. Campbell summarizes the following personal characteristics which may indicate the need for career changes during midlife—high achievement motivation, a generally steady and successful work record, high need for advancement, career challenge and individual satisfaction, psychological stability, positive self-image, high energy level, a sense of limited chances for advancement, and a sense of limited assistance in career preparation.[16] While many middle-aged persons change careers, a higher number do not because they already experience career and personal satisfaction. Others simply feel prevented from changing careers.

Some persons make new and challenging career choices during this midlife transition phase. Around age forty-five (the beginning of middle adulthood), many persons commit themselves to these choices and to

---

[14]Robert E. Campbell and James V. Cellini, "Adult Career Development," *Counseling and Human Development* 12 (June 1980): 8.

[15]Ibid., 8–9.

[16]Ibid., p. 9.

starting a new life.[17] The adult in midlife transition re-develops clear career patterns and makes a secure place in a career field.

AGE SPAN 50–60

Tips for Self-Assessment

- What do I need to do to hold on to my position since I am faced with younger competitors?
- To what extent is this lifestyle acceptable to me?

Most persons from forty-five to sixty have established themselves in their career field, but now they are concerned with holding onto their position.[18] At this stage, persons consciously make a decision about their lifestyle. Adopting a lifestyle influences a person's subsequent choices, but the selection of a lifestyle is not always conscious. Although you may choose or evaluate different lifestyles, you make such value judgements without knowing it. In fact, many aspiring persons are more concerned about their workstyle than their lifestyle.

Many difficulties face even those persons who keep their career and personal lives apart or who take on different roles in each. Because of limited time and energy, career problems can spill into family life or family life affect one's career. An individual's degree of dissatisfaction in one sphere of life can influence the other.

For many persons, middle-aged and older, family events often initiate a change in their work. Such changes primarily affect women because women have traditionally worked in the home or outside the home at a low-level position to supplement the family's income. The *empty-nest syndrome*—that stage in life when the last child leaves home—may be another factor encouraging women (and some men) to enter the marketplace. Persons may translate their empty feeling into an opportunity to return to school, adopt a new lifestyle, or enter a career. Divorce or death of a spouse may force an individual to return to work, to return to school for retraining, or to improve employable skills to enter a higher-level position.

Not all research indicates that women return to work during this stage. In a study of more than 5,000 women, Lois Banfill Shaw[19] discovered that women tended to re-enter to the labor market not as their nest emptied, but at the time when their youngest child was moving beyond the primary grades or into high school. Re-entry into the labor market after the empty-nest period had begun was less common than re-entry at an earlier

---

[17]Levinson, et al., *The Seasons of a Man's Life*, 279.

[18]Donald E. Super, "Vocational Maturity in Mid-Career," *Vocational Guidance Quarterly* 25 (December 1977): 294–302.

[19]Lois B. Shaw, "Problems of Labor-Market Reentry," in *Unplanned Careers: The Working Lives of Middle-Aged Women*, ed. L. Banfill Shaw (Lexington, MA: D. C. Heath, 1983), 33–44.

stage. Further, more women left the labor market as their nest emptied than entered it. Re-entry related both to the pressure of economic need, particularly when family income was low, and to the incentives provided by higher earnings potential. Shaw also learned that absences from the labor market of five years or longer did not penalize midlife women financially. Rather, she discovered, the loss in marketable skills was most pronounced during the first five years of absence.

Many middle-aged persons are searching for personal satisfaction. Men and women often make a career shift because they want to develop a new or long-standing interest which they had been unable to pursue before because of economic or family responsibilities. Other reasons for career change at this period could stem from experiencing dissatisfaction with a present position; desiring to improve social and economic status; desiring to work with different persons; avoiding a dead-end career; or seeking a stimulating and challenging position. Many persons during this age span enter early retirement as the result of, say, the termination of an educational or military career. Some elect to continue working, but remain retired from

Strix Pix

Retirement ages are
falling, and some take
to it very comfortably.

© Linda Ammons

Some individuals can choose to go on working productively at an advanced age.

their former career, while others prefer pursuing leisure activities now that they are retired. Many middle-aged persons never consider shifting gears to another career field or position.

LATE ADULTHOOD
(60 YEARS OF AGE AND BEYOND)

Tips for Self-Assessment

- Have I sufficiently prepared for my retirement years?
- Do I want to retire from my career?
- If I retire, what will I do to provide myself with sufficient personal satisfaction?
- Will the condition of my health allow me to do the things I care for the most?
- Although I want to retire from my work activities, in what manner might I continue doing similar career activities on my own time?

Social scientists predict that the average retirement age will continue to fall, so that by the year 2000, persons will be retiring at age fifty-five as opposed to today's retirement age of sixty-two or seventy. During this later stage of development, individuals either reach a period of satisfaction, contentment, and fulfillment or a period of meaninglessness, alienation, and loneliness. In the twenty-first century, many persons in this group are expected to be relatively healthy, educated, and desirous of more varied life options than those who are at the same age today. The retired will be looking for new work, as well as leisure activities. Persons living on fixed incomes may require work opportunities in order to supplement their incomes which have been affected by the high cost of living. Establishing part-time work may become seniors' career goals. As retirement eligibility along with retirement benefits become available to younger persons, they may leave full-time careers even though they are physically and mentally capable. Leisure time has become a myth for many retired workers, since their income is sharply reduced, and they are unable to afford most leisure activities. Such experiences they could better have afforded and enjoyed during earlier stages of development.

The individual facing the retirement stage must learn to adjust to a new situation—being unemployed. At this point, one's interests may move to the home or immediate community. Often, changes occur in security, health, and friendship patterns.

Around sixty-five to seventy, the pace of work may lessen, duties shift, or the nature of work changes. Many individuals seek part-time work.[20] For many age seventy-one and up, an end to their career occurs. For some persons their careers end easily and pleasantly; for others, the ending of their career is filled with problems and disappointments. Those who have prepared for retirement tend to experience little difficulty and disappointment and better adjust to this period.

REVIEWING CAREER PLANNING

Why do you choose one career over another, and what factors have the greatest influence on your decision? Some well-known writers believe that the choice of a career is determined by one's self-concept, which constantly shapes a person's self-image from childhood through adulthood. Other experts speculate that each human being must satisfy certain needs, and that continually we strive to meet those needs. In your case, you may have a need to achieve recognition; therefore, you will favor those careers which fill that need. In some cases, a person makes a career choice as the result of an accident or erroneous information. Unforeseen events or misfortune can lead to your settling for a career which is not necessarily your first choice. Still other factors, physical appearance, gender, and career availability, influence your choice. It is unlikely that any single factor will determine which career you eventually select; however, your ability to recognize elements having a negative influence will allow you to redirect your career decision-making.

[20]Donald E. Super and Jean Pierre Jordaan, "Career Development Theory," *British Journal of Guidance and Counseling* 1 (September, 1973): 3–4.

Once you recognize the need to make a career decision, you must set goals. Do not allow yourself to block out the need to organize this process of making sound decisions. For example, if you want to make good decisions, you must be aware of your preferences. Poor self-knowledge generally impedes your ability to define your objectives, or what you intend to achieve. An objective can be immediate, short range, or long range (e.g., immediate—getting part-time work; short-range—entering community college; long-range—becoming a medical librarian). After stating a clear objective, you can more easily make your career decision. Once you have gathered information and evaluated it, you can then judge the extent of risk involved in different decisions.

Your personal decision-making style will affect your career choice, and your awareness of this style can also help you improve the ways in which you make a decision. A sound decision almost always requires a systematic, step-by-step, and ongoing process.

Effective planning should include some knowledge of the career market. Understanding at least some of the ways the marketplace functions will help you make an informed selection of a career which interests you. As you explore, determine those careers which will meet your needs or give you the greatest satisfaction.

Assume that you have made some decisions about your career. Your next step is to identify employment opportunities which will enable you to start working toward career goals. Using both traditional and nontraditional approaches will enhance your chances of finding the best position. Researching opportunities may demand your continual efforts, in order for you to locate a position which will meet your career goals as well as the employer's needs.

Once you have identified some potential positions, how do you contact employers? First, you relate your skills, abilities, and talents with the job requirements. Second, you prepare a resumé, develop a placement folder, complete an employment application, and write a letter of application to directly contact the employer. You may find it appropriate to enlist expert assistance as you begin these tasks.

The employment interview is crucial in the hiring process. You must come to it well prepared to sell your services and skills to the interviewer or employer. Regardless of your qualifications, the effectiveness of your communication and interaction with the interviewer can determine whether or not you get the position. Applying positive perceptions and knowledge gained at the interview will also help your chances.

After you have accepted a position, your biggest concern is making a good start. Learning and applying good work habits will help you begin smoothly. Communicating with your employer, supervisor, and co-workers will enable you to establish good social relationships, which you will need in order to perform effectively. Without these communication skills, your chances of doing well will be limited.

As you continue to work in a position, you should consider ways to maintain your tenure and to develop on the job. You may need to devise strategies to obtain promotions and pay raises. Also, be alert to signs about the company which suggest you should seek employment elsewhere. Maintaining your career satisfaction is as important as performing your work well. The key to job satisfaction is to avoid stress, which may continue over long periods. Stress almost certainly will influence your behavior in the workplace and thereby your career progress and development.

Career planning continues even after you have settled into a position. As you grow and change, you need to determine whether or not your previous goals and accomplishments meet your present needs. New questions come to mind, such as "To what extent does my career allow me to contribute to society? Is my lifestyle in step with my career and vice versa?" Or, "I want to retire, take life easy, and enjoy leisure time with my husband and grandchildren, but can I afford to stop working at sixty-five?" These and other questions will influence your career planning and decision making.

Desire to move up the career ladder may produce discontentment or emotional conflict. A position which had been satisfying in the past may now be unacceptable. Any advancements which you might accomplish will only be a temporary success. After working successfully in a high-level career, you may see yourself still searching for a higher position. Your satisfaction will only be short-lived.

Conversely, you may not be weighted down with achievement. If so, you will likely be pleased once you have attained success in your chosen career. Some might label this behavior as lacking professional ambition; however, the behavior actually demonstrates having fulfilled your ambition. You no longer need to search for career opportunities.

Once you realize your goals, you have not completed the career planning process. You will continually make decisions and choices throughout your lifetime, which should be compatible with your aptitudes, interests, lifestyle, personality, character, and life goals. Career planning will be an ongoing experience to enable you to successfully perform your life's work.

POINTS TO REVIEW

1. Since career choice is not a single event, you should examine yourself throughout your development to determine what changes are occurring within you.

2. Career maturity is an ongoing developmental process. Your effectiveness in handling the tasks within each advanced stage of development will suggest your level of maturity.

3. Adult career development can be grouped into three general categories, (a) early adulthood, (b) middle adulthood, and (c) late adulthood.

4. Young adults must achieve several tasks before moving to a subsequent stage of development.

5. Young adults often follow the advice of a mentor, an experienced worker; however, this worker-mentor relationship needs to occur during or before middle adulthood.

6. During your early 30s, you question your achievements as well as the direction in which you are going, which both may result in some degree of turmoil. Eventually, you experience a need to *settle down* within a specific career field and apply your talents.

7. The task of the *settling down* period is to become vital within one's own setting and define a lifelong plan of self-direction.

8. Near the end of the 30-40 age span, persons may experience a strong sense of *being their own person.*

9. Being your own person usually includes breaking the young worker-mentor relationship and a desire to assume the mentor role yourself.

10. The *midlife transition* phase for many adults could be labeled as a *midlife crisis* or *midlife correction* period.

11. The midlife transition may or may not be a difficult experience.

12. Women, usually at about age 35, begin their midife transition. Midife may begin earlier for women than men and be more difficult.

13. Many adults during middle age express concern for the differences between their earlier career aspirations and their actual career attainments. As a result, some persons change careers.

14. Most middle-aged persons do not switch careers because of career and personal satisfaction.

15. The beginning of middle adulthood marks a sense of commitment, a career choice, and the starting of a new life.

16. Middle-aged persons, those 45-60 years old, usually have made a place in their career field, but many feel some concern for holding onto it, as well as holding onto an acceptable lifestyle.

17. The *empty-nest syndrome* may be a factor which encourages middle-aged parents to enter the career marketplace.

18. Many middle-aged persons retire early as a result of educational or military careers.

19. From age 65-70, persons may lessen the pace of work, shift their duties, or change the nature of their work to fit their personal interests and/or declining capacities.

20. Those who have prepared for retirement tend to adjust well to the late adulthood stage of development.

Experiential Exercises

1. Review the three career development stages. Then identify the one that you are entering or are now experiencing. Compare your own career development with characteristics of that stage.

2. Considering your own career development, describe the difficulties you have experienced and plans you have made within this stage.

3. a. How would you describe the level of satisfaction which your present career gives you?

   b. How would you describe any dissatisfaction you experience from your career?

c. Have you considered a career change? If so, what are the possibilities for such a switch?

d. Assume that you are strongly considering switching to another career. What steps would you have to make to accomplish this career move?

4. Your relationship with members of your family can affect your career performance.

    a. What factors about your relationship to your family seem to be the most pleasing and satisfying?

    b. Which factors inherent in your family relationships seem displeasing and unsatisfying?

    c. Do you want your relationships to your family to be different? If so, how would you proceed to make changes?

d. How is your present career meeting the needs of your family (providing satisfactory vacations, salary, working hours)?

e. If your present career is not meeting your family's or your own needs, what changes can you make to accommodate both your family and strong career performance?

5. Take a moment and think about what you value (things having real meaning to you). In what ways do your values differ today from what they were several years earlier?

6. Do you see yourself unable to engage in both leisure activities and career? If so, what can you do to change this?

7. What do you view as your greatest concerns? How can you change your lifestyle, including your career, to address these concerns?

8. List twenty leisure activities that you find enjoyable, meaningful, and worthwhile.

1.	11.
2.	12.
3.	13.
4.	14.
5.	15.
6.	16.
7.	17.
8.	18.
9.	19.
10.	20.

a. In which of these activities do you no longer participate? Explain why.

b. List other leisure activities which you might want to try.

INDEX